AUTOMOTIVE WOODWORKING

RESTORATION, REPAIR AND REPLACEMENT

ROLAND JOHNSON

MBI Publishing Company

Dedication

For Mom & Dad
Thanks for letting me follow my dreams.

Acknowledgments

Writing this book has been quite an adventure and a whole lot of work. No one can hope to write a technical manual without help. I would like to thank Steve Hendrickson for believing in the concept and encouraging me along the way, "just the facts Jack" Anatole Burkin for teaching me brevity, and the one person without whose help this book would not have been possible, my wife JoAnn. Thank you all for putting up with me.

I would also like to acknowledge Doug and Suzy Carr, Jim Dugué, John Lee, Warner Noble, and John Kirchoff for their help and encouragement.

First published in 2001 by MBI Publishing Company, Galtier Plaza, Suite 200, 380 Jackson Street, St. Paul, MN 55101-3885 USA

MBI Publishing Company books are also available at discounts in bulk quantity for industrial or sales-promotional use. For details write to Special Sales Manager at Motorbooks International Wholesalers & Distributors, Galtier Plaza, Suite 200, 380 Jackson Street, St. Paul, MN 55101-3885 USA.

Library of Congress Cataloging-in-Publication Data Available

ISBN 0-7603-0911-6

Edited by Pete Bodensteiner

On the front cover: The beautiful woodie in the foreground is a 1934 Ford belonging to Doug and Suzy Carr. Behind the Carrs' Ford is a Duesenberg body in progress. *Robert Genat/Zone Five Photo.*

On the back cover:

top: A slip joint is easy to cut and provides lots of gluable surface area to foster a strong bond between wood pieces. Here a rabbet plane is used to fine-tune a slip-joint tenon before assembly.

middle: Automotive woodworking isn't just for restoration. This 1932 Ford street rod has a beautiful, custom wooden body. *National Woodie Club*

bottom: Spokeshaves are great for removing wood on curved surfaces such as this quarter-window post.

About the Author: Roland Johnson is a professional woodworker who has owned his own woodworking business for more than 25 years. He has also enjoyed a life-long passion for anything on wheels. In 1995 Roland started writing articles for Fine Woodworking magazine and, to date, has written more than two dozen articles for the magazine, as well as articles for Rodder's Digest and Super Rod magazine. This book is a result of his love of wood, cars, and writing.

Contents

	Introduction	4
Chapter 1	Safety	5
Chapter 2	Wood, the Basics	9
Chapter 3	Tools	24
Chapter 4	Joinery: The Art of Making Big Boards Out of Little Boards	57
Chapter 5	Bending and Shaping Wood	76
Chapter 6	Making and Using Patterns	87
Chapter 7	Fasteners, Brackets, and Hardware	92
	Color Gallery	97
Chapter 8	Glue	113
Chapter 9	Repairing and Restoring Old Wood and Veneer	121
Chapter 10	Refinishing and Restoring Wood	128
Chapter 11	Finishing	134
Chapter 12	Building or Restoring a Wooden Body	142
Appendix 1	Sources of Supply	156
Appendix 2	Reference Books and Interesting Reading	157
	Glossary	158
	Index	159

Introduction

The purpose of this book is to instill in the reader a familiarity with woodworking as it relates to automobiles, and to allow the reader to use this information to build or restore a wood body or to restore wood body framing or interior trim.

The book is essentially two books combined under one title. The first part of the book is a basic woodworking manual that addresses the essential materials, tools, and methods used for building or restoring a wooden body or body frame. The second part addresses specific applications and techniques unique to automotive woodworking.

To write this book as a manual for a specific vehicle would limit the reader to methods and materials used for that specific body. I want the reader to be able to tackle any project, large or small, with the reasonable assurance of success through information. Building wood bodies or coachbuilding, as it has been referred to since real horsepower-propelled vehicles, is not any harder to accomplish than most other parts of an automotive project. Armed with adequate information and a few good woodworking tools the average craftsman should have no problem doing virtually any automotive woodworking.

Although it would be impractical to cover all the building methods used by manufacturers and coachbuilders through the years, I have tried to include representative methods, materials, and processes to help any builder or restorer through the toughest parts of a build-up or restoration.

This book is written for enthusiasts by an enthusiast. I am both an enthusiast of wood, having been a professional woodworker for over 25 years, and an enthusiast of automobiles, having reconstructed a number of cars over the last 30-odd years.

It is important to read this book completely and spend some time experimenting with the procedures before committing to a complex automotive woodworking project. It is essential to understand what a person is getting into before committing time and money to a project. Learning about the procedures and becoming familiar with the craft allows a person to be able to anticipate what work is required and in what sequence the work should be done. Appropriate tools and materials can be accumulated before they are needed so the project can flow smoothly. After reading this book, a person will also know how to estimate the cost of materials for the project.

Wood is wonderful to work with, and the results can be absolutely stunning. There are few things more beautiful than a brightly finished Carpathian elm burl dashboard in a Jaguar or the contrast between blond hard maple and deep cordovan Honduras mahogany on the flanks of a Ford V-8. The warm colors and soft contours that wood brings to an automobile are well worth the effort.

Even if you are not interested in building or owning a wooden-bodied car, a deeper appreciation of the materials, methods, and work involved can be acquired from reading this book. I always find that knowledge of a subject makes the enjoyment of that subject more complete and satisfying. Good woodworking!

Safety

Woodworking, like many aspects of automotive restoration, is inherently dangerous. This does not mean that injuries are unavoidable. I have been working wood for over 25 years and have suffered nothing more severe than an occasional sliver or minor cut. Even though woodworking involves the use of cutting tools that are capable of doing physical damage, serious accidents are unlikely if you use the tools properly and take normal precautions.

Knowledge is safety. Be sure you are comfortable with the operations you are performing. If using a certain tool or performing a certain process feels uncomfortable, find another way to do the work or spend some time becoming more familiar with the tool or process. The better you understand the operation of the tool or the steps of the process, the less likely you are to have an accident.

Practice on scrap wood. If you don't have scraps around your shop, stop at a local cabinet shop and offer to buy some of their scrap wood. You might even get the scrap for free. Working with scrap wood eliminates the worry of wasting valuable lumber should you make a mistake. When I am trying a new procedure or fabricating a complex piece from scratch, I often use scraps for a trial run. Once I am satisfied with the procedure and the results, then I commit to using the expensive furniture-grade wood.

Practice patience. Too often we find ourselves working with limited time. It's easy to lose one's patience when a process drags on and on. Hurry the project and you're more likely to hurt yourself or waste a lot of expensive wood. Fine woodworking is time-consuming, but in the end it is very rewarding.

SOME WOODS ARE TOXIC

The fine dust and oils of certain woods can cause allergic reactions in some individuals. Rosewood, as an example, can cause skin irritation or respiratory problems. I personally find black walnut to be a problem. Whenever I work with walnut, especially sanding or sawing the wood, I begin to feel as if I have suddenly contracted a mild chest cold. A few minutes of fresh air, and I begin to feel normal again. If you find that handling a particular wood causes rashes or respiratory distress, take precautions to avoid excessive contact with that wood.

SAWDUST IS A HEALTH AND SHOP HAZARD

Frequent inhalation of fine sawdust can cause respiratory problems. Sawdust is also a fire hazard. When you are working with wood, keep the dust contained with a dust collection system of some type or with a shop vacuum. A box fan in a window can help get sawdust out of the shop.

A shop vacuum can also be used to control sawdust created by woodworking tools. Here I have my vacuum connected to my router table using a homemade collector box mounted to the fence.

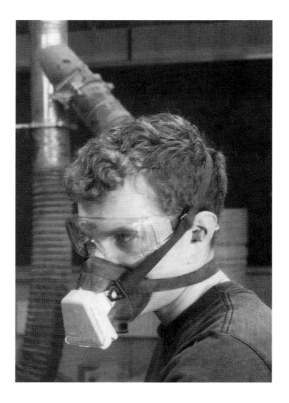

A good-quality dust mask will protect your lungs from potentially hazardous wood dust.

Clean up the work area when you are through for the day to help keep the sawdust contained.

When performing operations that create dust, wear a respirator. Inexpensive paper masks don't do a very good job of capturing wood dust. Invest a few dollars and buy a good respirator that has replaceable cartridges, similar to the masks used in body shops. A good respirator is comfortable to wear, won't steam your glasses (and everybody should wear safety glasses in the shop), and will last for years. High concentrations of wood dust in the air can be explosive. If you are going to do a lot of sanding, make sure there is a way of cleaning the dust out of the air or evacuating the contaminated air from the building. Wood dust is very pervasive and will get into and onto everything in the shop. If you have a gas- or oil-fired furnace or water heater in the shop, be sure to keep dust out of the burners. If your electrical panel is in your woodshop, keep the panel door closed to prevent dust build-up inside the panel, where it could cause a fire or explosion.

PROTECT YOUR HEARING

Routers, shapers, planers, and other woodworking machines create high levels of noise that can permanently damage your hearing. Damage to the ear from high noise levels is cumulative and not correctable. Wear good ear protection, preferably earmuffs, to protect your ears. I always carry a pair of soft plastic earplugs in my pocket for those times when my earmuffs are not close at hand. The soft earplugs work great for a day at the races too. Soft earplugs that are attached to a plastic headband are another alternative.

GLOVES ARE DANGEROUS AROUND MACHINERY

Resist the temptation to wear gloves for preventing slivers when you are working around machines. A glove can easily get caught in the rotating blades and knives that comprise most woodworking machinery. Don't for a moment think that you could overpower a blade or knife that grabs an errant glove. If a whirling cutter grabs a glove, a person doesn't have enough time to react. By the time you even realize what is happening, it is too late and the damage is done.

Gloves are OK when handling materials away from machinery, but once the tools are turned on, the gloves must come off.

LOOSE CLOTHING CAN CAUSE A LOSS OF FLESH

It sounds gruesome but the fact is that loose clothing can be extremely dangerous. Just like gloves, loose clothing can get caught and tangled in whirling knives or blades, and a person is just not strong enough or quick enough to be able to stay out of harm's way.

Never wear a long-sleeved shirt with the cuffs unbuttoned or rolled part way

Hearing protection is essential in noisy shop environments. Left to right: headband earplugs, soft earplugs, and earmuffs.

Earmuffs can be worn over safety glasses.

up. A dangling cuff is just asking to be caught by a saw blade or shaper cutter. Sweatshirts are my garments of choice when working around machinery. It is easy to push a sweatshirt sleeve up out of the way without a cuff dangling in harm's way.

If you wear a shop apron, as I do, make sure the apron strings tie in the back. Jewelry such as necklaces and bracelets don't belong in the shop. Even a watchband can be dangerous. I know folks who won't even wear a ring in the shop for

PROTECTION FROM CHEMICALS

During the course of building or restoring a wooden car, we have to deal with many chemicals. Any chemical can be dangerous if not handled properly.

Use a respirator whenever you are working with solvents and finishes. Filter cartridges are available for most common chemicals used in auto restoration, with the exception of methylene chloride–based paint stripper. There is no filter that will trap methylene chloride vapor. When using it, open the garage door or work outside with a good fresh air supply.

Wear latex or vinyl gloves when you are handling epoxies and finishing materials. Chemicals can easily invade your skin and end up in your bloodstream. Your kidneys and liver won't appreciate cleaning these chemicals out of your system.

Safety glasses worn over regular glasses offer full protection from flying splinters.

fear it may become entangled in a blade and drag their hand along.

Have great respect for the power of whirling blades and spinning cutters. They don't differentiate between flesh and wood.

PROTECT YOUR EYES

Always wear safety glasses when working in the shop. Wood splinters are sharp, and are often hurled with considerable force by machines. The next time you brush your hand across a piece of wood and get a small splinter in your hand, pause to consider how it would feel if that same splinter were lodged in your eye. If you wear prescription glasses, be sure to get lenses that are rated for impact. Better yet, wear a face shield as a second level of protection when necessary.

CHAPTER 2 TWO

Wood, The Basics

Wood is an incredibly strong, versatile, and easy-to-work material, whose strength can only be destroyed by decay and fire. While it is impossible to work-harden wood, it can, however, be overstressed to the point where the fibers will separate, resulting in fractures and failure. Using the correct wood and proper joinery techniques can limit the possibility of fracture or failure and provide a strong structure that could last for centuries.

Wood is what I consider a "live" material. By that I mean that wood is constantly moving and changing shape. Changes in temperature and humidity affect the moisture content of wood, and that may cause wood to shrink, expand, twist, cup, and warp. The higher the moisture content of

wood or its surroundings, the more likely wood will move, a result of hydraulic action in the wood's cells. There are no adhesives, fasteners, or brackets that can stop wood from moving, but wood may be joined and attached in such a way to allow it to move without causing problems.

The way a tree grew and the way it is sawed into lumber also affect wood movement. Your success at automotive woodworking will also be enhanced by knowing a little about which species of woods are appropriate for what applications and why. Not all woods are necessarily good choices for use in an automobile.

HOW A ROUND LOG CAN BE FLAT SAWN

Woodworking terminology includes the terms flat sawn, rift sawn, and quarter

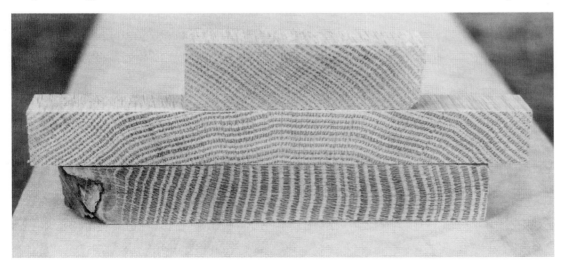

Here are three types of grain orientation. Top to bottom: rift sawn, flat sawn, and quarter sawn.

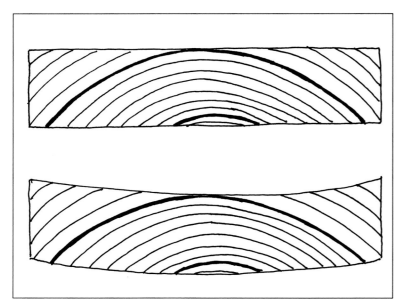

Longer annual rings have more surface area than the shorter annual rings, and they shrink more, which results in the board cupping.

WOOD MOVEMENT IS CAUSED BY WATER

Wood movement follows set patterns. Wood will behave in predictable ways as it gains or loses moisture. Most wood shrinkage occurs tangential to the center of the tree. In other words, the annual rings represent lines that the board will shrink along. If a board is flat sawn, the annual rings will be longer on one side of the board (when viewed from the end of the board). As lumber dries, the longer annual rings will shrink more than the short annual rings. This uneven shrinkage results in what is referred to as cupping. As the longer rings shrink, the board becomes narrower on that surface. (See illustration.)

Of course there is shrinkage from the center to the outside of the tree, but this shrinkage is proportionately a lot less and therefore not as critical in determining wood movement.

Quarter-sawn wood is the most stable type. Quartered wood has the shortest and most consistent annual rings, which results in very minimal and uniform shrinkage. Rift sawn is next in line and, ironically, flat sawn is the least likely to remain flat.

sawn. Flat-sawn wood, sometimes referred to as plain sliced, has the annual rings parallel to the wide surface of the board. Rift sawn has annual rings that are from 30 degrees to 60 degrees to the wide surface of the board. Quarter sawn has annual rings that are 45 to 90 degrees to the wide surface of the board. (See illustrations.)

This is where the three types of grain orientation are found in a log.

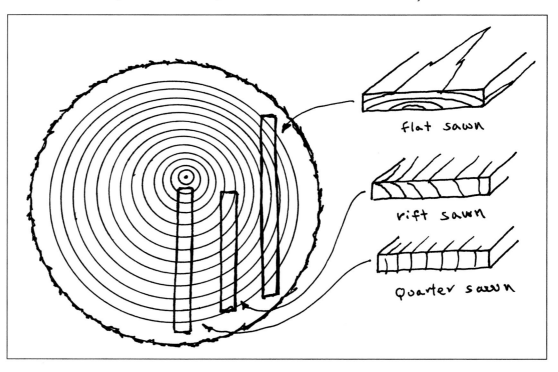

flat sawn

rift sawn

quarter sawn

EVEN "DRY" WOOD CONTAINS WATER

The water present in wood is referred to as moisture content or MC. Moisture content is measured as a ratio of the weight of water in the wood to the weight of the wood when it is baked bone dry. The moisture content of wood varies from season to season, according to the locale. In the northern half of the United States, where we have humid summers and dry winters, wood MC will follow the weather, losing moisture in the winter and gaining it in the summer. These seasonal changes, which cause wood movement, need to be accounted for when constructing a wooden-bodied car. Doors that have adequate margins around the perimeter in a dry shop in the dead of winter will bind and be hard to operate at the car show in the middle of the summer.

A tool called a moisture meter can be helpful in determining the moisture content of wood. A moisture meter uses electronics to accurately "read" the wood. (For more information on moisture meters, see chapter 2.) The tool is a good investment if you have any concern that the lumber you are buying may not be adequately dry. A lot of work can be wasted if you work with wet lumber, which will dry out after construction and leave you with gapped or warped and twisted parts.

If you don't want to buy a moisture meter, there's a simple method for determining moisture content in wood. Cut a small chunk off the end of a board and weigh the piece. Then place the piece in your kitchen oven at low temperature. Remove the wood every half-hour or so and weigh it; repeat until the weight doesn't change. To determine the moisture percentage, subtract the bone-dry weight from the original weight and divide the remainder by the original weight. For example: If you have a piece of wood that weighs 16 ounces before drying and stabilizes at 14 ounces, it has lost 2 ounces of moisture. Divide the 2 ounces by 16 and you will arrive at 12 percent moisture content. (Keep in mind that the wood near the end of a board will be drier than the rest of the board because the exposed end grain dries faster than face grain.) This method of determining MC will only be approximate for the whole board, but it will get you pretty close.

KILN-DRIED VERSUS AIR-DRIED WOOD

Air-dried lumber is wood that has been dried by simply storing the wood out of the weather in an unheated building or under a roof or cover of some type. Air-dried wood will reach equilibrium with the outdoor atmosphere of a particular area. In the Midwest, this means the wood will be in the range of 12 to 15 percent moisture content. The MC needed for woodie wood is 6 to 8 percent, which is what furniture makers consider appropriate MC for wood they use.

Drying air-dried wood to furniture grade means the wood needs to be subjected to an atmosphere that is drier than the natural humidity in the particular area. This can be done by storing the wood in a heated building with low humidity, the usual shop atmosphere, but it takes quite a while for the wood to lose that last few degrees of moisture to become dry as furniture grade. If you have air-dried lumber and the time to dry it to furniture grade, read up on lumber drying and give it a try. It is not particularly hard to achieve but there are specific steps, such as how you stack the lumber, that must be followed or you may ruin the entire batch. If you have the air-dried lumber and don't have the time or facility to complete drying it, take it to a wood kiln. Ask around and make sure the wood kiln operator has a good reputation. Rushing the drying process may ruin your wood.

There are several types of kiln-drying procedures used by wood producers. The most popular method is the steam kiln. In a steam kiln the temperature is raised to around 170 degrees, for hardwoods, and held at that temperature to speed drying. Steam is introduced into the kiln to help slow the evaporation of free water in the wood, keeping the lumber from being overly stressed. If the wood is dried too quickly, honeycombing occurs. Honeycombing is a type of fracture of the woodgrain, ruining the wood. I find that wood dried in a steam kiln is not particularly strong. It is unsuitable for steam bending or laminate bending and breaks easily on short-grained pieces. Wood dried in steam kilns is used extensively in the millwork and cabinet trade, but I prefer wood that has been dried by slower and more gentle means.

Dehumidification kilns dry the wood by drawing the moisture out of the cell walls. By lowering the humidity in the kiln, water leaves the cell walls through osmosis. This process is slower but much kinder to the wood structure. The cell walls remain intact, and the wood retains its original strength.

Wood may be dried by simply stacking it in a heated enclosure fitted with fans for air circulation. This is a low-tech system that can be used by anyone. The heat source can be solar, electric, gas, or whatever else is available. Careful monitoring of the humidity in the enclosure and proper air circulation will result in well-dried wood. This method is fairly slow and if the heat is too high or the humidity too low, damage such as honeycombing can occur.

The easiest way to get well-dried wood is to buy it from a good hardwood retailer. Ask how the wood was dried and avoid steam-kiln dried wood if possible.

WARP AND TWIST

Rough lumber is rarely perfectly straight, and may suffer from warp, twist, cup, kink, bow, and crook. To be better able to discuss wood and its problems with professionals, following are explanations and illustrations that define these terms.

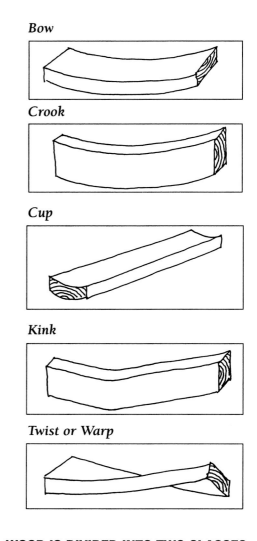

Bow

Crook

Cup

Kink

Twist or Warp

WOOD IS DIVIDED INTO TWO CLASSES

Wood is commonly classified as hardwood or softwood, yet not all hardwoods are hard, nor are all softwoods soft. Hardwood is a botanical term that is used to describe a group of trees that are broad-leaved and usually lose their leaves on a seasonal basis, referred to as deciduous. Softwood is a botanical term that refers to a group of trees that have needles or scalelike leaves, such as the arbor vitae that surround many homes, and are typically evergreens, which remain green year-round.

SOFTWOODS

Pine, spruce, and fir are the major softwood species that are available commercially. There are quite a few different subspecies of pine, but the best pine for automotive use is southern yellow pine, both longleaf and shortleaf. Eastern larch (tamarack), western larch, and hemlock lumbers are a bit hard to find in many commercial lumberyards, but they are very strong. Hemlock was used for the floors in pickup boxes for years because of its strength, which is comparable to oak, and its low cost. Fir tends to split easily and the splits tend to run out along the grain; it's best left for the building trade. Spruce, especially Sitka spruce, has long been used in "stick and rag" aircraft construction, due to its light weight relative to its strength. Good quality spruce is expensive; since weight is not a critical factor when building a car, spruce isn't economically viable. Cedar works great for canoes, and redwood is the ultimate wood for rot-resistant decks, but both of these woods are a bit too soft for the abrasive environment of automotive usage.

Generally speaking, softwoods are not ideal woods for automotive use. The soft wood and short fibers will not hold fasteners well, when subjected to vibration and torsional stresses. If you want to use softwood for interior work, such as seat frames or floorboards, I would suggest southern yellow pine.

Buy your softwoods from the same lumber dealer that sells good quality hardwood. Furniture and millwork makers are much fussier about the wood they use, and quality dealers will stock the wood they and you need.

Inexpensive softwood is good for mocking up the body before committing good wood to the project. It is also good for practicing joinery procedures, although it does not cut or machine as nicely as good hardwood.

TROPICAL WOODS

In the last decade or so a lot of tropical woods have shown up in hardwood lumberyards. Tropical wood is often hard to keep stabilized in our North American climate, which experiences extremes of temperature and humidity. Some species, such as mahogany and rosewood may do fine, but unless you have personally seen good results, I would avoid using them. Solid exotic wood may lend an exotic appeal to your project, but tropicals may also lead to massive problems if they prove to be unstable and the movement results in doors and window frames twisting and warping. An exception to my rule would be the use of exotic wood in veneer form. Laminated onto plywood, most tropical woods should be acceptably stable.

HARDWOODS

I would like to explain a little about the different types of pores in hardwood that make up the texture and grain of the wood. Ash, oak, and elm are common hardwoods and are known as ring-porous. These woods have distinct differences in the size of the pores between the early grown wood and the late grown wood in each annual ring. This difference creates the pronounced uneven grain that makes the appearance of these woods so distinctive. Maple, cherry, birch, basswood, and poplar have pores that are evenly distributed throughout the annual ring and are referred to as diffuse-porous. Most domestic diffuse-porous woods have relatively small pores, resulting in grain that is subtle and hard to distinguish. This is an important consideration when choosing wood for your project. If you want the framing of a wooden vehicle to be very homogenous and character-free, choose a diffuse-porous wood such as maple. If you prefer a wood with a pronounced grain, then select a ring-porous wood such as ash. I will limit my discussion of hardwoods to the species that have traditionally been used to build car bodies. I will also mention a few species that will work well for utility use, such as upholstery backers and for constructing patterns. And finally, I'll tell you why some species won't work particularly well as woodie wood. Here we go.

Ash (White—*Fraxinus americana*; green—*Fraxinus pennsylvanica*)

In my opinion, ash is the best wood for automotive use. Ash is very resilient and has a great "memory," which means it will return to its natural form even after being bent under load. Ash is easily steam bent for curved pieces and is also a good choice for laminate work, where thin strips are glued up into curved forms (For more information on bending wood, see chapter 4.) Fairly rot resistant, ash tends to weather well, turning a light gray color if left unfinished. With a good finish, ash turns a rich honey-gold color as the wood oxidizes from exposure to sunlight. Ash has a very pronounced grain, similar to oak, and looks great as framing for maple or mahogany panels. Ash frames make great armatures for sheet metal, and ash is still used by at least one contemporary car builder: Morgan Motor Company of Malvern Link, Worcestershire, England, for its body frames.

Ash is readily available throughout the United States and Europe. There are several different species of ash, with white ash being the most commonly available and most widely used in woodie construction. Green ash is indistinguishable from white ash and the two are often confused. Oregon ash and European ash are essentially similar to white ash. Black ash is easier to identify by its slightly darker color and physically lighter weight and is seldom used in automotive work.

Aspen (*Populus tremuloides*)

Aspen is a great utility wood. It may be distinguished from other fine-grained and light-colored woods by telltale green streaks. Aspen is inexpensive and will work great for upholstery backing, blocking, braces, and brackets.

Basswood (*Tilia americana*)

Basswood has long been a favorite wood for pattern making and carving. Very finely grained and reasonably soft, basswood cuts cleanly and easily with sharp chisels or knives. Basswood is physically very stable, making it ideal for use as a substrate for veneer. Lightweight and fairly flexible, it is often used for the strips that cover the top bows in woodie tops.

Birch (*Betula spp.*)

Birch is easily confused with hard maple because it is very similar in color, grain patterns, and weight. Birch is used for millwork and cabinetry, but I have never seen it used for woodies.

Butternut (*Juglans cinerea*)

Butternut is in the same family as black walnut and is sometimes referred to as white walnut. Much softer than black walnut but with similar grain patterns, butternut's light tan color makes it a very desirable trim wood. Butternut will dent about as easily as pine, so it is best to use it where it won't see a lot of physical contact.

Beech (*Fagus grandifolia*)

Very similar in color and weight to hard maple, beech is rarely used in American woodies, although it has seen use in Europe and England for bodies and body frames.

Cherry (*Prunus serotina*)

Often referred to as a fruitwood, cherry has a light reddish brown color when new, and with exposure to sun the color turns deep reddish brown. Long prized as a premium furniture wood, cherry lends itself well to interior trim work but would not be durable enough for exterior use.

Cherry has a very distinct color difference between the sapwood and heartwood of the tree. For uniform color, this sapwood is usually discarded. Cherry is fairly expensive, and if you have to throw a lot of sapwood away it can become *very* expensive. Make friends with your lumber dealer and pick the heartwood cherry, even if you have to pay a premium to get it.

Elm (*Ulmus rubra*)

Red elm works well for almost any aspect of automotive woodworking. Also known as slippery elm, it has a pleasing reddish brown color and a grain that is similar to red oak or ash. Red elm is a good candidate for steam or laminate bending. With such a pleasing grain and color, red elm would make wonderful interior trim.

One drawback to red elm is its limited availability. Dutch elm disease wiped out most of the large red elms in this country. Specialty hardwood dealers usually stock or can get red elm, but in some areas of the country it is practically nonexistent.

Hickory (Carya ovata)

I included hickory just because I have heard rumors of the extensive use of hickory in woodie bodies. It must be some kind of folktale, because I have never actually seen it used that way nor has any reliable source confirmed its use in a woodie body. Hickory is extremely strong and springy, but it is hard, heavy, not much fun to work with, and tends to twist and warp easily. I think hickory is best left for chair rungs and ax handles.

Mahogany, Central American mahogany (Swietenia spp.)
African mahogany (Khaya spp.)

Long regarded as a premier furniture wood, true mahogany (*Swietenia spp.*), often referred to as Honduran or Central American mahogany, is easy to work, highly rot resistant, and beautiful to boot. Ribbon-stripe African mahogany makes beautiful interior and exterior paneling. Deep reddish brown, mahogany contrasts strikingly with ash or maple framing. Both of these mahoganies are readily available from specialty hardwood dealers.

Interior trim made from mahogany is pleasing to the eye, and it holds up well in use. Bright finished (high gloss) mahogany has long been a staple of elegant sail and powerboats, and it brings that same charisma to automobiles.

Mahogany, Philippine (Shorea spp.)

I have included this wood under the commonly used name Philippine mahogany although the correct name is lauan. It has been referred to as Philippine mahogany for so long that most people identify it with that name, more than with the name lauan.

Usually available at do-it-yourself lumber dealers, Philippine mahogany is not related to the more expensive African or American mahogany and is too soft to be of any automotive use. Lauan is often sold in plywood form, and it works great for drawer bottoms and cabinet backs, but it has no place on a woodie body. I have seen nicely constructed woodies with lauan paneling and it ruins the looks of an otherwise nice car. It is a shame to spend so much time and effort to restore or build a car only to ruin the finished product by trying to save a few dollars on materials.

Maple (Acer saccharum)

One of the most widely used woods for woodie bodies, hard maple (also known as rock maple or hard rock maple) is very dense and heavy. Often referred to as a white wood, maple is very dent and abrasion resistant, and will hold screws very well. The even color and subtle grain of maple results in a more uniform look to wood body framing. Combined with dark mahogany paneling, the result is a body of exquisite beauty.

The biggest drawback of maple is its lack of rot resistance. Maple left unfinished and in high moisture conditions will rot surprisingly fast. I am sure there were many woodies framed in hard maple that experienced serious rot just a few years after they were built, and that is one of the reasons so few survived. Water entering the woodgrain around a screw or bolt will quickly encourage fungi to grow, staining and damaging the wood quickly. Some of the old literature from woodie manufacturers recommended varnishing the wood body twice a year, and I suspect few owners followed those guidelines.

Properly varnished and cared for, maple will last for decades and gain a beautiful golden patina over time. Hard maple machines nicely, although due to the high sugar content in the wood, it will scorch easily if your tools aren't razor sharp.

Maple, soft (*Acer saccharinum*)

Similar in appearance to hard maple, soft maple is lighter in weight, slightly more gray in color, and is quite a bit softer physically. Dimensionally stable, easy to work, and stronger than softwood, soft maple is ideal for upholstery backing, brackets, and many other utility uses.

Soft maple is not a good candidate for exterior use.

Oak, red (*Quercus rubra*)

Red oak would not be my choice for wooden body framing. More brittle than ash, red oak also has high concentrations of tannic acid, which will cause the wood to develop black stains if it comes into contact with ferrous metal and water.

Many re-creations of depot hacks and other woodies may be found that have been built of red oak, but I think this was more a result of easy availability of the wood. I would leave red oak to the kitchen cabinet makers.

Oak, white (*Quercus alba*)

White oak is very rot resistant and would hold up well to abrasion and denting. The drawback with white oak is the tannic acid contained in the wood. As with red oak and walnut, black staining will occur when white oak comes into contact with ferrous metal and water.

White oak would be an unusual but interesting choice for a woodie, with its subtle grain, which resembles ash. Quarter-sawn white oak would give a car a very exotic look because of the large and pronounced flake patterns found throughout. A body built of quarter-sawn oak would resemble some of the fine antique oak furniture that was so highly prized in the United States early in the twentieth century, sort of like a rolling roll-top desk!

Quarter-sawn white oak makes an outstanding choice for interior trim.

Teak (*Tectona grandis*)

I thought I would include teak in this discussion just because it has been used as a trim and deck wood in boats for so many years. Teak is quite hard and has a very high silica content, which is very abrasive to cutting tools. Extremely rot resistant, teak can be left unfinished and exposed to the elements for a long period of time without fear of decay. It is also very resistant to the detrimental effects of salt water.

Teak is expensive and probably not particularly suited to automotive use unless you plan to leave the wood on your car unfinished and expose it to surf spray. In this case the wood body will outlast the rest of the car!

Walnut (*Juglans nigra*)

Walnut is a favorite of woodworkers. Deep chocolate brown with pronounced grain, walnut is well suited for trim work, dashboards, and many other automotive applications. Walnut is very rot resistant and is hard enough to wear well in automotive usage, although I have never seen a body made of walnut. The dark color could make quite a statement if combined with curly maple or bird's-eye maple paneling.

Walnut contains high amounts of tannic acid and turns black when brought into contact with ferrous metals and water. Best to keep walnut indoors and dry.

There are many more species of wood available through hardwood lumber dealers, but these are the woods that I have personal experience with. They have historically been used in the manufacture of wooden-bodied cars.

SPECIALTY WOODS AND VENEERS

There are many exotic woods that are either extremely rare, or they are not readily available in solid-lumber form. Veneer makes it possible to use these exotic woods without breaking the bank or getting the tree huggers up in arms. A single 1-inch-thick board can produce up to 64 sheets of veneer. A log that would have produced a few hundred square feet of lumber can produce many thousands of square feet of veneer.

Wood that is normally unstable in board form can be tamed when reduced to veneer. Burls that are fragile as solid wood can be veneered onto a stronger backing, making the burl strong enough to withstand the rigors of everyday use.

Here is a list of my favorite specialty woods. These woods can make incredible trim and dashboards when veneered over a suitable substrate such as basswood, soft maple, or high quality plywood.

Buy your veneer from a reputable dealer and always buy more than you think you need. The exotic nature of the veneer makes it almost impossible to match the color and grain if more veneer is needed for the project. I have often ordered more than double the amount I thought I would need for a project and never regretted having the extra wood—at times I needed every inch of that extra veneer.

Carpathian elm burl

This particular burl species has been used by Rolls-Royce, Jaguar, and many other top coachbuilders to veneer dashboards, window frames, and other interior embellishments.

Wild grain patterns and beautiful colors ranging from light tan to deep reddish brown make elm burl a favorite of furniture makers. It is, without a doubt, one of the most beautiful and unique woods in the world.

I would like to someday build a small, elegant woodie with all of the exterior panels veneered in Carpathian elm burl. Although it would take a fair amount of work to make custom veneered panels, the result would be well worth the effort. It is my favorite exotic veneer.

Mahogany, flame crotch

Slicing the crotch where two branches diverge in a tree produces flame crotch mahogany veneer. Feathery in appearance, flame crotch mahogany has a wonderful translucence that produces the illusion of depth. Available only in veneer, flame crotch mahogany can be used to create an incredible dashboard or console. It is at its best when used on large surfaces where the entire grain pattern can be seen. This is not a good wood for novice woodworkers, however. I have used crotch mahogany on several projects and it is difficult to keep flat and to keep it from cracking.

Maple, bird's-eye

Bird's-eye maple describes its appearance in its name. Small "eyes" in the grain produce an exotic appearance and has a translucence that adds depth to a flat surface. Highly prized by cabinetmakers, bird's-eye maple in solid wood or veneer can greatly enhance the interior of any car, and it is especially appropriate for a wooden-bodied car.

Because of the swirl of the grain around the "eyes," bird's-eye maple is hard to stain. Dye is the best way to change the color of the wood but I prefer the natural wood's color, which will gain a golden patina as it ages

Maple, curly or fiddleback

This wood is a favorite of instrument makers who use it to form the body of a fiddle, hence the name fiddleback. Tightly packed "waves" of grain appear to have a curly texture and depth when in reality they are flat. This ability to refract light and give the appearance of false depth is one of the wood's unique qualities. Finished without staining, curly maple will gain a deep golden appearance in a relatively short period of time from exposure to sunlight. Curly maple would be outstanding as a veneer for window frames and other interior trim pieces.

Pomelle sapele

Dark, chocolate brown with grain patterns resembling turbulent water, pomelle sapele is a very extravagant-looking wood. Its ability to literally bend the light reflected off its surface makes for an incredible material that is one of my all-time favorites.

These are my favorites and represent just a few of hundreds of veneers available. (See Sources of Supply.)

BUYING WOOD

A few tools are necessary when you go to purchase wood. A tape measure, pencil, paper, and hand-held calculator are the basics. A small hand plane, such as a block plane or a bullnose plane, and a flashlight will greatly help "see" the board, especially in dimly lit surroundings, such as a lumber storage warehouse. It's a good idea to ask for permission before you take a shaving with a plane, which will help reveal the true color and grain of a rough-sawn board. A moisture meter (see chapter 2) is a real asset even if you are buying wood from a reputable dealer. A lot of lumber on the market is not adequately dry. A

moisture content (MC) of less than 10 percent is what you want. A pair of leather gloves will save your hands from splinters while sorting through the lumber.

The first rule in purchasing wood for your project is to avoid the discount home improvement stores. Although they may carry hardwood lumber and plywood, it will not be the quality you are looking for. Most of these stores do not stock lumber in sizes thicker than finished 3/4 inch, and you will never find rough-sawn, furniture-grade lumber there. And last, but certainly not least, is the support and help available at these stores. The employees of home improvement stores are not hardwood experts and won't provide the kind of information needed by a cabinetmaker. After all, that is what we are building: rolling cabinets.

Before you set off to buy lumber, do your homework. Know the common and botanical name of the wood you are seeking. Make a list that includes overall board footage and any unusual size requirements. Knowledge is power, so know what you are talking about. Demonstrating knowledge of wood, wood terminology, and also a genuine interest in getting the best lumber will go a long way toward the success

Here is a "wood-buying kit" consisting of a moisture meter, calculator, flashlight, measuring tape, low-angle block plane, pencil, note pad, and gloves. The moisture meter, shown with the meter's wood species moisture chart, is an essential tool for determining the moisture content in boards.

of your project. A top-quality car can't be built without top-quality lumber.

Try to find a lumber dealer who will allow you to sort through the lumber pile and pick the pieces that look alike. Seek out boards that match in color and grain. Be sure you leave the pile neatly stacked and be courteous to the yard employees. A poorly stacked lumber pile is not only a hassle to deal with but can ruin the lumber. Those yard employees are your allies in the search for the right wood. Explain what you want and what you are going to do with the wood, and they can direct you to the right pile and may even know where the really special stuff is stashed. And remember, be nice!

If you are really lucky, you might find a dealer who specializes in flitch-sawn lumber, or lumber that has been sawn through and through and has the boards kept in the same order as when they were a whole log. This type of lumber guarantees consistent color and grain throughout the stack. The price will be significantly higher for flitch-sawn lumber because of the special handling involved, but if the project is really special, the price will be justified.

Rough-sawn lumber is the best. Surfaced lumber will save the hassle of flattening, straightening, and smoothing the boards but it also limits a person to specific dimensions. Additionally, with rough-sawn lumber, the extra thickness can be put to good use. If you do not have a jointer, table saw, and planer, then surfaced boards are what you need to buy unless you are skilled with hand planes and have a lot of energy and time at your disposal. A complete body could be built using nothing more than a couple of good handsaws, several hand planes, and a good set of chisels, but it would be time consuming. Rough-sawn lumber allows a person to see if there is a natural twist or warp to the board. Stay away from any lumber that is gray or weathered looking, as it has not been adequately protected from the elements and will have unacceptable flaws.

GRADING LUMBER

Lumber is sold in a confusing array of different grades. Hardwoods are graded differently from softwoods and the grade standards have changed over the years. Grading takes into account knots, cracks, and other surface defects. There are tight knots and loose knots, end checking and surface checking, and other defects that can degrade a board.

Since the average automotive project does not utilize much softwood, I will be brief with the softwood grading parameters. The best grade of softwood commonly available in most lumberyards is referred to as D Select. The allowed defects in D Select are small pin knots or other abnormalities such as fine checks or light pitch spots. These types of defects will not affect the strength or surface integrity of the wood.

Less than select grades are referred to as 1 Common, 2 Common, and 3 Common. The 1 Common and 2 Common have tight knots and other defects and the 3 Common will have loose knots and is considered "utility" grade. Most of the common grades are "S-dry" meaning the moisture content will be in the 18 to 20 percent range. Common grade softwood is good for shop projects but not desirable for automotive woodworking.

Hardwood is graded by a different set of parameters that include width of board and percentage of waste in a board.

First and seconds (FAS) is used to describe the best-quality hardwood boards. Less than 16 percent waste, which might include flaws such as end checking and bark edge, is allowed with an FAS board and one face must be clear. The boards have to yield a minimum 3-inch-wide by 7-foot-long cutting. The moisture content will be at furniture grade, which is 6 to 8 percent.

Select and better is the next step down from FAS. Select and better allows slightly smaller minimum yield and allows one side of the board to be graded as Number 1 Common. Lately I have found some hardwood dealers using select and better as a replacement for FAS. Select and better is not as good as FAS!

Number 1 Common has knots and short lengths but is still dried to furniture grade MC. Up to 33 percent waste is allowable with 1 Common.

I have seen FAS lumber that has been anything but top quality. There are other considerations such as mineral streaking, grain run-out, and the general look of the grain that are not taken into account by lumber graders. A board that has no knots but wild grain and odd markings is of little use in a top-rate project. If I can get by with short lengths of finished board, I often find myself buying Number 1 Common because of the beauty of the wood. Let your eyes be the guide to wood grading. I just purchase a lot more wood so I can cut around the defects and use the clear parts. An added bonus to using Number 1 Common is that it is considerably less expensive.

The biggest concern in buying Number 1 Common is the moisture content. Although the standards call for furniture-grade MC, in reality Number 1 Common is often insufficiently dry. Be sure to test the wood with your moisture meter, and if it is above 12 percent MC don't buy it.

When I order lumber that will be picked by the yard and delivered to me, I always ask for FAS grade. I also specify minimum width and length so I don't end up with unusable lumber. This does not mean that all of the wood will be acceptable for my project, but at least I know I stand a better chance of getting usable lumber than if I were to order Number 1 Common. Wood that is unsuitable for your project can always be returned to the lumberyard if kept in the same condition as when it was delivered. It is a good idea to order extra lumber so you can pick and choose for grain and color.

SAPWOOD IS FOR SAPS

Sapwood is the soft outer wood on the tree. In many species it is distinctly different in color and texture from heartwood. Sapwood typically rots more easily than heartwood because it is the section of the tree that transports the nutrients, which makes a favorable environment for hungry fungi, the leading cause of rot.

Avoid sapwood or purchase enough extra lumber and cut away the sapwood. In most cases sapwood is easy to identify because it is significantly lighter colored, often white or light tan.

Sapwood is the lighter-colored wood on the edge of a board. These examples of cherry (top) and walnut (bottom) show the extreme color difference between sapwood and heartwood.

CALCULATING BOARD FEET

Rough-sawn hardwood lumber is sold in random widths and lengths but in specific thicknesses. It is sold by volume, or by the board foot. One board foot is equal to a piece of stock 1 inch thick by 12 inches wide by 12 inches long.

At the lumberyard you will find hardwood grouped by species and thickness, measured by quarters of an inch. A 1-inch-thick board is called a 4/4 (pronounced four-quarter) board, a 1-1/4-inch board is called a 5/4 (five-quarter) board, and so on. These dimensions are for rough-sawn lumber and are approximate. Normally a 4/4 rough-sawn kiln-dried board will measure 1-1/8 inches thick. The boards are cut a bit thick to compensate for differences in shrinkage during the drying process. Suffice it to say that if you buy a 4/4 board, it will be at least 1 inch thick.

One board foot of lumber equals 144 cubic inches of rough stock. For example, if you are buying a board that is rough sawn, 1 inch thick (4/4), 7-1/2 inches wide and 8 feet long, you would have 5 board feet (b/f) of lumber. (1 x 7.5 x 96 divided by 144 = 5) If you are buying a 3-inch-thick (12/4) board that is 6-3/4 inches wide and 105 inches long, you would have 14.76 b/f of lumber. (3 x 6.75 x 105 divided by 144 = 14.76) This is a standard throughout the industry and makes it very easy to price lumber accurately.

Pricing is usually described as dollars per thousand board feet or $/M. For example: Ash is currently selling for $2,250 per thousand or 2,250/M. The price per foot is $2.25. For a piece of ash wood like the example above, 14.76 board feet, the cost would be $33.21. Now you see why a pencil, paper, and a calculator are necessary when buying lumber !

Example 1: 4/4 x 12-1/2-inch x 105-inch board. How many board feet?
1 x 12.5 x 105 = 1,312.5
1,312.5 /144ci = 9.11 b/f
9.11 bf x $3.25/ b/f = $29.60

Example 2: 5/4 x 8-1/4-inch x 96-inch board.
1.25 x 8.25 x 96 = 990
990 /144ci = 6.875 b/f
6.875 b/f x $4.50/bf = $30.94

A fraction-to-decimal conversion chart is a very handy thing to carry along if you can't remember that 3/8 equals 0.375 or 9/16 equals 0.5625. There are also calculators available that will work with fractions of an inch.

STORING WOOD

Now that you have made an investment in the raw materials for your project, the lumber must be stored properly. Wood is a perishable commodity and must be treated as such.

To prevent damage, lumber must be stored in such a way that all the boards receive adequate air circulation. Moisture can ruin good lumber quickly. Fungus is the main destroyer of wood, and allowing wood to become damp and stay that way gives fungus an ideal place to grow.

When you stack your lumber, place stickers between the stacks. Stickers are small strips of wood. I make mine 3/4x3/4 inch x 48 inches long from scraps or offcuts of the same species of wood being stacked. The stickers are placed at right angles to the stack of boards. Space the

Stickering lumber for good air circulation is critical for drying wood or keeping wood dry. Stickers should be placed one directly over the other for equal weight distribution throughout the pile.

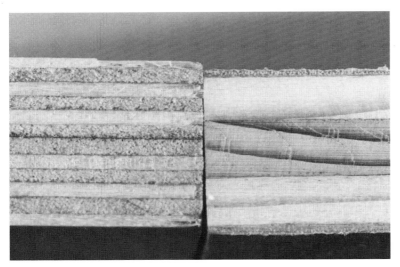

Baltic birch plywood (left) has more layers of wood than regular construction-grade plywood (right), resulting in more dimensional stability.

stickers about 2 feet apart and keep the stickers one above the other as the stack is piled so that loading pressures are evenly distributed down through the stack. The stickers allow for adequate air movement around the wood, which will keep moisture from accumulating between the boards. Make sure you also leave room between the boards on each stack to allow air to circulate up through the stack.

Keep your lumber in a dry location and away from direct or bright sunlight. My wood storage rack is on the north wall of my shop, well away from any window. I prefer to store my main lumber supply in an unheated, well-ventilated building. I bring the lumber I am going to use for a project into my shop a week or so before I intend to use it so the lumber can acclimate itself to the shop temperature and humidity before machining.

Never stack wood directly on the floor, especially if the floor is concrete. Use timbers to hold the lumber up off the floor. Make sure the timbers are level so you don't induce warping of the wood. Wood that is unevenly stacked and left for a length of time will assume twists and warps. If you are storing the wood on a dirt floor, put down a plastic tarp before you start the pile. The tarp will keep ground moisture from reaching the wood. A level, well-ventilated lumber stack will keep the wood in excellent condition for years.

PLYWOOD COMES IN MANY VARIETIES

Plywood is a manufactured board composed of an odd number of layers or plies of veneer joined with an adhesive. The plies are arranged in a crisscross fashion so that the grain of each adjacent ply is oriented at 90 degrees, which results in a panel that is dimensionally stable, flat, and stronger than solid wood. The face ply, which may be either hardwood or softwood, is usually of a higher-grade veneer than the back ply or center plies. The more layers of veneer in a plywood panel, the more stable the resulting panel will be.

Hardwood and softwood plywoods usually both contain softwood core plies. An exception is plywood known generically as Baltic birch. Also referred to as Finnish plywood, this product is hardwood plywood that is composed of many thin plies of void-free hardwood veneer, usually birch, that is resin bonded. This is a premium plywood, and I recommend it for any structural plywood use or veneer substrate.

When plywood is framed with solid wood, you end up with a panel that is strong and lightweight, the perfect characteristics for a wooden-bodied vehicle. Thin plywood can be bent into slight compound curves, such as the body panels in a 1950 Ford woodie, resulting in complex shapes that can be achieved with simple methods and materials.

Most lumberyard plywood is best suited for construction use. Construction-grade plywood is usually lower grade with voids in the center veneer plies. These voids weaken the plywood. The exposed void makes a weak edge and can collect water. I use construction plywood for floorboards and shop jigs. I use Baltic birch for all other panel needs such as seat and console frames. Baltic birch hardwood plywood is usually available from larger lumberyards and hardwood lumber dealers. It is expensive when compared to construction plywood, but well worth the extra money.

Choose plywood that is resin bonded and marked exterior or marine grade.

Plywood that is not exterior grade will not hold up to the moisture and temperature changes a car body is subjected to, even if it has a good finish on it.

If curved plywood panels are needed for a project, laminate several layers of thin plywood around a curved form. Bending plywood is available for such applications and differs from regular plywood in that it has thinner plies and utilizes wood that is flexible. Some bending plywood actually has all of the ply grain running in the same direction to make it bend easier. If the radius is gradual standard, 1/4-inch plywood will often work, but make sure the plywood is good quality and resin bonded.

Be aware of the fact that most plywood does not measure as labeled. Plywood that is supposed to be 1/4 inch is, in fact, nearer to 3/16 inch. The same goes for other thicknesses. Before cutting rabbets or dadoes, measure the actual plywood to be used and make adjustments to your machine setups. Loose-fitting plywood is hard to secure, hard to finish, and will look shabby.

The face veneer on plywood is available in two different cuts, rotary and flat sawn.

Rotary veneer is veneer that is peeled from the log in one continuous sheet as the log is turned against a knife. Flat-sawn veneer is sheared from the log as boards are sawn from a log. Rotary veneer tends to have wild, unnatural looking grain, while flat-sawn veneer looks just like normal boards. Rotary cut is less expensive than flat sawn and is good for uses where the veneer won't show. If the plywood is visible, flat-sawn plywood will give the look of solid wood.

I have seen woodies on which the panels were made from rotary-cut plywood, and the resulting look is odd at best. For a few dollars saved the resulting project was significantly downgraded.

When you buy plywood for body panels, buy sheets that were produced at the same time so that the grain pattern will match. Most good lumber dealers can supply consecutively veneered sheets.

If you can't find plywood sheets that were produced consecutively, try to match the color and grain as closely as possible. Make sure you have good, natural lighting when comparing the sheets so you can see the true colors.

This picture shows the difference between rotary-cut hardwood plywood (left) and flat-sawn plywood (right, also called plain-sliced plywood). The bold grain patterns of rotary-cut plywood are not as attractive as the flat-sawn variety.

Tools

I love tools. My wife accuses me of being a woodworker just so I can collect tools. There may be a bit of truth in that, but the fact is, without appropriate, well-tuned, and good-quality tools, finished work may suffer, if it gets done at all.

I have seen well-intentioned hobbyists try to replace the wood in a car body using cheap, inappropriate, and poorly tuned tools. Often they end up walking away from the project frustrated and disappointed in the results of their hard work. Such discouragement can lead to a complete abandonment of the project.

Woodworking is not the black art many auto enthusiasts think it is. A modest selection of good hand and power tools will make most woodworking tasks easy to accomplish. Woodworking is just another set of rules to learn, like welding, wiring, or rebuilding an engine. Learn the tools and the techniques, and woodworking will become another skill that will make building and restoring cars a little easier.

One of the best tools a person can have is access to information. Join a local woodworking club. There is a wealth of information just for the asking in these clubs. Join the National Woodie Club, an organization specific to wooden cars. There are lots of great sites on the Internet that can help solve woodworking problems. A lot of the folks involved with these institutions have run into and solved the same problems you are bound to encounter. You'll find most of them willing to help you around those pitfalls. Knowledge is power, and you can tap their power.

MOISTURE METERS

A moisture meter is a tool that doesn't cut, shape, or sand wood. It can't drill a hole or make a joint. A moisture meter can't do any real woodworking, and yet it

A moisture meter is an essential tool for every woodworker. The one shown here is measuring the moisture of rough-sawn white ash.

Gossamer-thin shavings are the product of a sharp hand plane. Planing wood by hand can be enjoyable as well as productive. This is my "hot rod" Stanley Number 4, equipped with a Hock blade and a Clifton cap iron.

is one of the most important tools you can have in your shop.

A moisture meter is a relatively inexpensive tool that can save a lot of money. Wood is expensive and, if you value your time, labor is costly, too. Investing a lot of money in wood and labor, only to have your work undone by excessive moisture in the wood, can be very distressing. Dry wood is essential for good results, and the quickest way to determine your wood's moisture content (MC) is to use a moisture meter.

There are a number of different brands of moisture meters on the market. All of them will do an adequate job of measuring the moisture content of 3/4-inch-thick lumber. The lowest priced hobby meters are best suited to measuring the moisture content of small-dimension wood such as trim and narrow, thin boards. But since the average woodie uses some fairly thick lumber, it is a good idea to invest in a more sophisticated meter. Meters come in two types. One is an electrical resistance type that utilizes a pair of sharp pins to "read" the wood. The pins will create small holes in the lumber. The meter measures the electrical resistance between the pins and shows the reading on a scale that corresponds to the percentage of moisture. The second type of moisture meter uses electromagnetic waves to measure moisture content. This type doesn't have pins and won't mar the wood. I prefer the nonintrusive

style, and use a Wagner L606 model, which does a very good job of keeping me out of trouble. I am usually measuring the MC of my parts right up to the final assembly to make sure all of the parts have similar MC. I really appreciate the fact that I don't have to poke holes in my finished parts to get an accurate MC reading.

Keep in mind that moisture meters can't accurately measure the MC in the center of thick lumber. The readings will only be accurate for the first inch or so of depth, so any wood thicker than 2-1/2 inches will not be measured completely. The reading, however, is still a good indication of how dry the wood is.

HAND TOOLS

You may wonder why I've devoted so much text to hand tools. That's because hand tools are still the best tools for accomplishing many woodworking tasks. In fact, all of the woodworking required to build a complete car body can be done with hand tools.

Machines such as planers, table saws, band saws, shapers, and jointers are great for surfacing and dimensioning rough boards and molding profiles with speed, accuracy, and ease of effort. Hand tools are a better choice when you must cut complex joinery, shave that last curl of wood for a perfect fit, or remove waste material on compound-curved surfaces.

Hand tools are a pleasure to use. A finely tuned hand plane can remove a lot of material in a hurry with minimum effort and without a lot of noise and dust. There are few things as satisfying as watching gossamer-thin shavings curl out of the plane's throat, covering your workbench with the quiet work of a moment's effort. There is a Zenlike communication between the operator and the tool. Hand tools remind us that we practice our hobbies for relaxation and pleasure.

An added benefit is the relatively low cost of hand tools, especially if you do a little scrounging at garage sales, auctions, or antique shops. Many of these old tools have better-quality steel and castings than their modern counterparts. A lot of work can be accomplished without investing a fortune in power tools, and hand tools take up a lot less space.

There are many books devoted to old hand tools. I have listed a couple of sources for these books in Sources of Supply. If you are serious about wanting to get the best tools for your money, pick up a couple of these books and familiarize yourself with the brand names of the good tool companies. Keep in mind that just because a tool is old doesn't necessarily mean it's good. There were many poor quality tools produced in the last century or so. A little research can help you identify the good tools at flea markets, auctions, and antique shops. Tool catalogs are also a good source of information and offer descriptions and uses of the tools.

ESSENTIAL WOODWORKING TOOLS

If a person has never done any serious woodworking, outfitting a shop for a wooden car project can get expensive. It is not that the tools themselves are expensive. Rather, without a lot of woodworking experience a person often buys tools he or she doesn't need, seldom uses, or are inappropriate for the task ahead. I have compiled a couple of lists of what I consider essential tools, including a basic starter set that can be used to perform most of the woodworking operations needed to build a wood body. There are many tools that are nice to have, or can save lots of time, but my lists pare the tool selection down to the basics, for those of you who are just getting started with woodworking and do not want to spend a fortune. A rule of thumb to keep in mind is that good-quality used tools are a better buy than cheap new tools.

Hand tools
Crosscut saw
Dozuki saw
Coping saw
Bench chisels
Spokeshaves (flat and curved sole)
Low-angle block plane
Scrub plane
Smoothing plane
Nicholson Number 49 or Number 50 patternmaker's rasp
8-inch four-in-hand rasp
10-inch round smooth rasp
10-inch smooth cabinet rasp
Shavehooks (usually sold in a set of three)
Carving mallet
Dead-blow hammer
Sandvik scraper blade
Combination mortise/marking gauge
A very good set of straight-blade screw drivers
Board sander
Block sander
Good-quality square (I prefer Starrett; expensive but worth the money)
Sliding T-bevel
Diamond sharpening stone, medium grit.
Tapered drill bits with countersink and adjustable depth stop

Power tools
Band saw (minimum 12 inch)
Router, at least 2 horsepower
Router table
Cordless drill

One of my favorite layout tools is a Starrett 6-inch double square; it's very accurate and handy for laying out tenons and other joinery.

Jointer
Jigsaw
Table saw
Drill press
Mortising attachment for drill press
Portable belt sander
Orbital sander

Use these lists as a guide to assembling the basics. More detailed descriptions of the tools follow. Again, I want to stress the need to buy the best-quality tools you can find or afford. Don't be afraid of used tools.

MEASURING AND LAYOUT TOOLS

Good measuring tools are absolutely essential. A square that isn't square or a tape measure that is slightly "long" will result in nothing but frustration and can cause serious problems. Buy good-quality measuring and layout tools. It's money well spent.

I prefer a rather small tape measure, a 12-foot Stanley, as opposed to the big, clumsy contractor's tapes. The big tapes are designed to be able to extend over 8 feet without support for measuring house framing. You won't need that for automotive restoration; the added bulk of a big tape just gets in the way.

A good 4-foot straightedge aids layout work and is a good tool for checking flatness and alignment. And, of course, you will need an accurate combination square, framing square, and my favorite layout tool, a Starrett 6-inch double square; it is goodness and light in a small package.

A sliding T-bevel is an absolute necessity when working with odd angles, which is what woodies are all about. The sliding T-bevel can be set to any angle and locked in place with a wing nut or cam clamp. The tool is essential for transferring angles from patterns to the new wood or for determining angles on original pieces.

Sliding T-bevels are essential for laying out or determining angles. They are a must-have for automotive woodworking, in which there are lots of angles!

Checking a Square

To check the accuracy of a square, use a straight-edged piece of plywood and mark a line along the square.

Flip the square over and check the square against the drawn line. If the square is true, the lines will match perfectly. This is a quick way to check a square before buying, or after rough use such as repeated meetings with the floor.

Here is a little tip on how to quickly check a square for accuracy. Joint a wide board or piece of plywood straight along one edge. Take your square and mark a line up from the squared edge. Now flip the square over and compare the edge of the square to the line. The back edge of the square and the original line should match up. If there is a gap between the ends of the lines, that gap is exactly double the distance your square is out of square. You can use this method for checking a square you are about to buy if the store also sells plywood or has a square-edged counter available.

A mason's string line is handy to have around when you start assembling the wood body. Many woodies don't have much body framing that is square or plumb, and a stretched string creates a straight reference line to take measurements from. A string stretched down the middle of the body will assure that everything ends up centered on the car. It is all too easy to build things crooked if you don't have a good point of reference.

HAND PLANES

When a person thinks of woodworking hand tools, the first tool that often comes to mind is the bench plane. Bench planes have long been the workhorses of hand tools. Used for dimensioning and joining wood, bench planes are an essential part of hand woodworking.

Before I explain the types and uses of planes, a short description of the parts and names of a plane will help keep us all on the same page. The main body of a plane is like a foot; it has a toe, a heel, and a sole. The device that supports the blade (also known as an iron) assembly is referred to as the frog, and it sits directly behind the throat of the plane. It is attached to the body of the plane by a pair of screws and can be adjusted for fine-tuning the cutting action of the plane. The frog also contains a depth-adjustment wheel and a lever, for lateral adjustments of the iron. The iron is attached to a cap iron by means of a short, large headed machine screw. The iron and cap iron are attached to the frog by a lever cap. The rear handle of the plane is often referred to as a tote, while the other handle is simply called a front knob. Smaller planes such as block planes and molding planes share the same terminology but not all of the same parts. Block planes, for example, do not have a frog, and the mouth is adjusted by means of a movable plate ahead of the mouth in the sole of the plane body. Whew—that's a lot of minutia! But if you grab a plane and take it apart, the function of all these parts will become self-evident.

During this discussion I will use Stanley planes as examples, as well as Stanley's numbering system, which many other plane makers have adopted. Stanley has long made some of the best, affordably priced planes available. Old Stanley tools have developed quite a well-deserved following by woodworkers and tool collectors.

Bench planes come in a variety of sizes with specific uses for each size. The largest planes are called **jointer planes** (Stanley Number 7) and have a long sole and are quite heavy, which aids in taking heavy shavings and control. Jointer planes are used for squaring and truing the edge of a board. A jointer can also be used to flatten a board because the plane's long length lets it float over the low spots and trim the high spots, just like the board sander a body man uses to level filler.

Scrub planes (Stanley Number 40) are narrow, lightweight planes with a large, fixed throat opening that allows coarse shavings to pass through. The iron is thick, narrow, and curved at the cutting edge. Because of this narrow, curved iron, scrub planes can remove a lot of wood in big hurry with surprisingly low effort. The

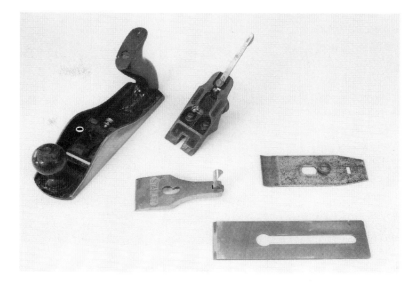

results are lumpy and rough, but there are few tools that can remove a hump or twist in a board quicker.

The **jack plane** (Stanley Number 5) is literally a jack-of-all-trades plane. The sole of a jack plane is long enough that it will do a reasonable job of leveling a surface or truing an edge. The plane is heavy enough to do a good job of removing large amounts of wood and when well tuned will do a decent job of finish planing.

Smoothing planes (Stanley Number 4) are designed for doing the final surface smoothing. A finely tuned smoothing plane will leave a glass-smooth finish and put in skilled hands can plane figured wood, such as bird's-eye maple or curly ash, with little or no tear-out of the grain.

Here are a hand plane's parts, clockwise from left: plane body, frog, cap iron, blade (also known as the iron), and lever cap.

Planes can transform wood from rough sawn to satin smooth. They can flatten a surface, straighten an edge, and shape a curve. Here is a good selection of wood planes, clockwise from top right: scrub plane, curved-sole spokeshave, flat-sole spokeshave, Stanley No. 75 bullnose rabbet plane, Stanley No. 90 bullnose rabbet plane, Stanley No. 4 smoothing plane, Stanley No. 5 "Jack" plane, and Stanley No. 7 jointer plane.

The block plane is the open-end adjustable wrench of the wood planes. From left to right, here are a Stanley 09-1/2, a Stanley 60-1/2 low-angle, and an antique Stanley 118 "schoolboy" low-angle block plane.

My favorite plane is the **block plane**. Available in two different styles, regular and low angle, the block plane is the open-end adjustable wrench of the hand plane family. A properly tuned block plane can do a very good job of smoothing small pieces, shearing the end grain on a tenon, fairing the face or edge of a curved board, or any of a multitude of delicate planing jobs. This is the plane that I keep readily at hand for those little tune-ups that make the difference between an OK job and perfection.

The block plane removes wood much faster than a rasp or coarse sandpaper and leaves a glass-smooth surface. The low-angle block plane (Stanley Number 60-1/2) was originally designed for cutting end grain. The low angle of the blade shears the fibers, rather than tearing them, and leaves a smooth finish on end grain. It will work very well on difficult wood such as curly maple. I have a low-angle block plane that I have "hot-rodded" with an af-

termarket Hock blade. The Hock blade sharpens better and holds that edge much longer than the stock blade. (For Hock blades, see Sources of Supply.)

If you have only one plane in the shop, make it a low-angle block plane.

A **rabbet plane** is designed with one or both sides of the mouth open to the sides of the plane body, which allows the iron to cut the full width of the plane's sole. This feature is especially handy when trimming the shoulders on tenons or rabbeting a groove on the edge of a board. Rabbet planes are available in a variety of sizes, pitches (the angle of the iron), and configurations. My personal favorites are the Stanley Number 90 and the Number 92, both small enough to be used with one hand.

A **spokeshave** is basically a small metal plane that is very short and has handles on the sides. The short sole on the plane makes it easy to get into tight areas and also makes the plane easy to control. The handles on either side of the blade create a tool that is easy to maneuver over curved or irregular surfaces. A spokeshave is ideal for shaving the narrow edge of a board, especially a rounded edge. While it's not the easiest tool to learn to use, the spokeshave can, with a little practice, perform amazing feats of wood removal.

The biggest problem most rookies run into with the spokeshave is extending the blade for too deep a cut. Before making a cut, take a piece of scrap wood, clamp it in a vise, and start shaving the edge with the spokeshave. Adjust the depth so that the

The difference in angles is shown between the low-angle block plane on the left and the regular block plane on the right. The low-angle block plane works better on end grain and difficult hardwoods.

Spokeshaves are great for removing wood on curved surfaces such as this quarter-window post. The flat-sole spokeshave is best for outside curves and flat surfaces, while the curved-sole spokeshave is ideal for inside curves.

tool doesn't dig into the wood but takes clean shavings. I take a practice cut on scrap nearly every time I adjust the blade. I get no surprises that way.

There are two types of spokeshaves: flat sole and curved sole. The flat sole spokeshave is for shaving flat and convex surfaces. The curved sole is for shaving concave surfaces and the inside edge of curved pieces, such as brackets. They are both necessary tools to have when you are shaping curved or rounded wood.

Record makes wonderful spokeshaves, made of malleable cast iron. Nearly unbreakable and inexpensive, a pair (curved and flat sole) should be in every shop.

HANDSAWS EXCEL AT FINE JOINERY

Handsaws are an important part of every good woodworking shop. Power saws are great for cutting wood quickly, but there are times when a handsaw is better, especially for fine joinery. Handsaws create a lot less dust and noise and are quite inexpensive when compared to the cost of a power saw. There are handsaws designed for almost every type of wood cutting. Buy high-quality saws. The steel is better, and they stay sharp a lot longer than inexpensive saws.

Keeping a saw sharp is very important. As soon as a saw's teeth become even a little dull, it will be hard to keep the saw cutting accurately. The effort needed to cut the wood will be higher, and it is hard to keep the blade on line when more physical effort is needed to saw the wood. Dull teeth also create a ragged cut, because they tend to tear the grain rather than shear it.

Make your saws slippery. I used to wax my handsaws with car wax years ago. It worked great for keeping them slick, but silicone in the wax would sometimes get on the wood's surface and cause finishing problems. Candle wax and carnuba wax work well. You can also buy specialty coatings designed for saw blades that will keep them slick.

A **crosscut saw** does exactly what its name implies, it cuts across woodgrain. A crosscut saw has teeth that are shaped for shearing or cutting the grain. When made with good-quality steel and freshly sharpened, a crosscut saw can make short work of cutting the hardest wood to length.

A crosscut saw (top) has smaller teeth, which are shaped differently from ripsaw teeth (bottom).

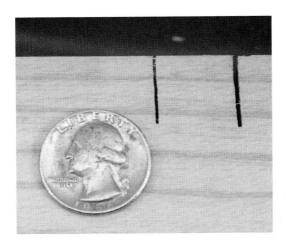

Here you can see the difference in kerf between a Japanese Ryobi saw (left) and an American backsaw (right).

A **ripsaw** is used to cut a board to width, sawing along the grain. Traditional ripsaws have fewer and larger teeth than a crosscut saw. The teeth are designed to scrape or plane the wood away and the large gaps, or gullets, between the teeth help clear the shavings from the cut.

A traditional American-style saw cuts on the push stroke. Cutting on the push stroke tends to make the saw blade chatter because the blade is compressed a tiny bit as each tooth digs into the wood, especially at the start of the cut. As the tooth shears the wood fibers, the compression is

released, causing a tiny vibration. This isn't a big problem unless the saw is dull or has a thin blade, such as a tenon saw. When a saw binds in the cut, the chatter can become excessive and make it difficult to cut a clean, straight line.

Japanese-style saws cut on the pull stroke, which tensions the blade as it cuts through the wood fibers. There is virtually no chatter with a pull-stroke saw and a very thin blade can be used without the problems associated with compression chatter. Imagine trying to push a thin wire through a tight-fitting hole, versus pulling that same wire through the same hole. It is also easier to use the mechanical advantage of your weight when pulling a saw. Your arms don't need to do nearly as much work, and you can use your legs and torso to help.

Japanese saws also have a unique tooth shape that cuts more aggressively than traditional American saws. It's really amazing how fast a Japanese saw can cut hardwood with little effort on the sawyer's part. My favorite Japanese saw is the **Dozuki** saw. A Dozuki has a thin blade that is ideal for fussy joinery, such as a dovetail, and it will rip cut quickly. It will also crosscut quickly, leaving a nice, clean surface. I use my Dozuki saw almost exclusively when handsawing. It will cut to a line with little effort

A Japanese Ryobi saw (top) cuts on the pull stroke, while an American backsaw (bottom) cuts on the push stroke. The backsaw is so named because of the reinforced back edge of the saw blade.

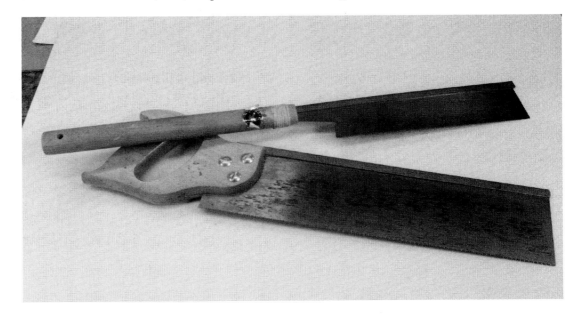

and great accuracy. Many Dozuki saws have replaceable blades, so it is easy to keep them dead sharp by simply replacing the blade as soon as it dulls. Keep a replacement blade on hand, and you will never have to suffer with a dull saw.

Many furniture makers prefer to use a **dovetail** saw for cutting precise joinery. A dovetail saw, also known as a backsaw because the blade has a reinforced back edge, has very fine teeth and a thin blade ideal for cutting joinery. There are many styles and sizes of dovetail saws, and a snoop through a good tool catalog can show you what is available.

There are some new hybrid saws on the market. These saws combine the traditional push stroke with Japanese-style teeth for a more aggressive cutting action. I have a couple of them in my shop and they work great for quick rough cuts, but not for fine work. There are a couple of hybrids on the market that combine a traditional backsaw with Japanese-style teeth. I haven't tried one so I don't know how well they work.

CHISELS

Bench chisels are an indispensable part of any tool chest. It is a good investment to buy the best-quality chisels you can afford. A good set of bench chisels will hold a sharper edge longer than an inexpensive set.

I use Marples blue-handled chisels. Reasonably priced with nearly indestructible handles, these chisels hold a sharp edge reasonably well. More expensive chisels usually have better steel, which will hold an edge even longer.

When using a chisel there is one rule I always follow: never raise the mallet more than 3 inches from the handle when driving the chisel. Any farther and you are using excessive force. Either sharpen the chisel or slow down. A chisel that is driven with such force is not well controlled and can do more damage than good. Brute force will not compensate for impatience or a dull chisel.

If you are really into having the right tools for every job, buy a set of mortise chisels. These chisels have a heavier blade designed for prying the waste wood out of a mortise. During the course of wooden-car building you will cut a lot of mortises. A bench chisel will also do a good job of cutting mortises, but a couple of my old chisels have a slight bend from prying too hard while roughing out big mortises. This was not the tool's fault, just impatience.

RASPS AND FILES

A good rasp can remove a lot of wood in short order with complete control over the shape of the work. Half-round rasps are the rasps that I use most for shaping. They can work efficiently on flat or curved stock. A four-in-hand rasp has both curved and flat, fine and coarse faces, literally four rasps in one. This rasp can do rough work quickly and then proceed to smooth the surface nearly to the sandpaper stage.

Rasps can range from large-toothed, aggressive cutting to small-toothed, fine cutting. Try to assemble a variety of shapes and tooth sizes. You can never have too many rasps when it comes to shaping wood.

Files are better at removing metal than they are at removing wood. Because of the way files are designed, they tend to plug easily with wood dust. A good double-cut file will still do a very nice job of detail filing. I have a double-cut bastard that I have

Here is my motley set of rasps and files. My favorites are my tapered mill bastard file that I'm holding and the four-in-hand next to it.

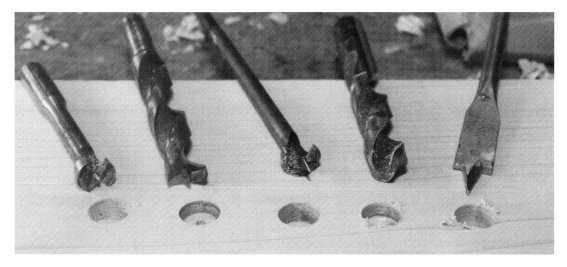

This shows drill bits and the holes they are capable of boring. From the left are a Forstner bit, spur bit, power bore bit, twist bit, and spade bit.

modified for detail work, and it is a tool I wouldn't want to be without. I modified the file by grinding a curve along the back of the file, narrow at the end, wide at the tang. The smooth, curved back works well for straightening molded lines and edges without the problem of cutting into the adjoining surface.

SCREWDRIVERS

Buy a good set of straight-blade screwdrivers. Buy the best you can find. There is nothing more frustrating than having the blade of a screwdriver give up and chew the heck out of the screw slot just as you get the screw tight. Worse yet, a deformed blade is prone to slip, which can result in a nasty gash in the wood.

Forstner bits are adept at boring overlapping holes, and are great for boring mortises.

DRILL BITS

Drill bits are an important part of woodworking. Selecting the appropriate style of bit depends on the application and the size of the hole.

Forstner bits are designed to drill smooth, flat-bottomed holes with no tearout at the rim. They are ideal for drilling through veneer, figured wood, and any place where a very clean, smooth hole is required. Forstner bits have a small center spur that allows accurate placement of the hole and a razor- rim that guides the bit, as well as cleanly slicing the wood. Two flutes remove the bulk of the wood. The sharp rim, rather than the center spur, guides a Forstner bit, and that allows you to drill overlapping holes without chatter—good for drilling mortises. (See chapter 3.) Forstner bits are also very good at drilling at steep angles.

Forstner bits aren't without problems, however. Because they don't have flutes for waste removal, the bit has to be withdrawn from the hole often to clean the chips out. Otherwise the bit can literally become stuck under the packed waste wood. It's a small price to pay for such accuracy.

Forstner bits can be purchased in sizes ranging from 1/16 inch to 2-1/8 inches in diameter. They are for use with wood only. Buy a good-quality set, as the cheap bits dull quickly and are a pain to sharpen.

Multispur bits are similar to Forstner bits except they have spurs around the rim. Spur bits are good for larger-sized flat-bottomed holes and through boring.

Multispur bits are usually available in larger sizes, up to 3-1/8 inch in diameter, making them a good bit for drilling gauge holes in a dashboard.

Brad-point drills feature two knife-edged spurs and a central brad point on a twist bit. The knife edged spurs shear the fibers of wood, resulting in a cleanly bored hole, while the twist removes the waste. The brad point centers the drill, making it easy to accurately start the hole.

Brad-point drills are commonly available in sizes ranging from 1/8 inch to 1 inch in diameter, in 1/16-inch increments.

Power-bore bits are similar to Forstner bits in that they have a center point, two cutting flutes, and a spur to shear the wood fibers. They are cheap cousins, however. Power-bore bits do an adequate job of boring a clean hole but not quite at the level of a Forstner bit. Because of the lack of a continuous rim to guide the bit, power-bore bits can wander in the wood. The best use of these bits is in the drill press.

Power-bore bits are available in diameters from 1/4 inch to 1 inch. These bits seem to be getting hard to find in tool stores.

A **spade** bit consists of two flutes and a centering point on a flat spade at the end of a round shaft. If they are dead sharp they can cut a reasonable hole, but are really designed to be cheap, disposable construction bits where speed is of the essence and quality of the hole is secondary. Keep a set around the shop to do the dirty work, so you don't have to use your good boring bits. Spade bits are available in sizes ranging from 1/4 inch to over 2 inches in diameter.

The **taper drill/countersink combination** bit is one of those truly great inventions. The tapered twist bit mimics the shape of a wood screw and drills a hole that allows the screw to grip along its entire length. The built-in countersink makes drilling screw holes a one-tool operation.

Forstner bits will also bore angled holes, leaving a clean rim in the process. The Forstner also leaves a flat bottom in the hole.

There are taper drill/countersink bits available with adjustable stop collars. This tool drills a tapered hole and countersinks to a preset depth in one operation. Taper drills come in sizes corresponding to screws. Buy a Number 6, Number 8, and Number 12, or shoot the works and buy a complete set.

Twist bits work very well for drilling into end grain. Compared to all of the other woodcutting bits, twist bits drill the fastest, cleanest, and most accurate holes in end grain. The drawbacks to twist bits are their tendency to walk at the start of a hole, they are hard to get started at severe angles, and they have a tendency to tear the fibers at the perimeter of the hole. To help solve a couple of these problems, I regrind the V-angle of my twist bits. The most common V-angle is 118 degrees, which is ideal for drilling metal. There are 90-degree bits available from specialty tool houses, but I prefer to grind mine even shallower than 90 degrees. I have a few

The twist bit on the left has had the point reground at a steeper angle for more of a shearing cut. The modified bit cuts cleaner and faster in wood than the original one.

A good set of hole saws is handy to have around the wood shop.

The toothed rim does the cutting, allowing a hole saw to bore big holes at an angle.

smaller-sized bits ground to roughly 60–70 degrees, and they cut like crazy. (See photo.) This bevel helps the drill bit center itself, and the flute angle cuts the wood fibers cleaner and faster.

A **self-centering drill** is handy to have for installing hardware, hinges, and brackets. A self-centering drill has a guide that

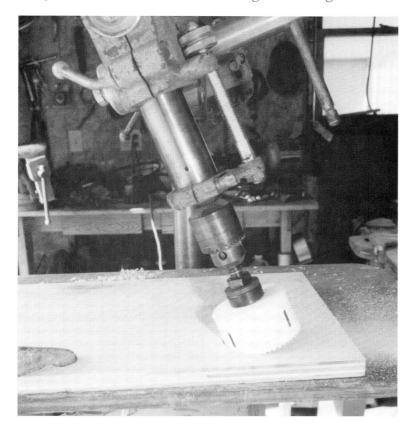

locates the drill bit exactly in the center of the hole in a hinge or bracket. As the hole is drilled, the guide slides up the drill bit, allowing full-depth drilling. This tool utilizes a standard twist bit, which is easily replaced when it becomes dull or broken. The most commonly available brand is the VIX bit, available from most woodworking tool outlets. The bit is sized according to approximate screw size. I have a Number 5, Number 9, and Number 12 bit, and they seem to fill all of my needs.

HOLE SAWS

Hole saws work well whenever there is a need for a large hole through a board. They work great for cutting holes for gauges and switches in a dashboard, for cutting large access holes in floorboards, and other applications where a hole cut completely through the board is desired. Hole saws will also cut clean holes in iron, steel, aluminum, and plastic.

A drill press is still the best power source for a hole saw. It is also easy to cut an angled hole through wood because the cut is supported around the rim, allowing a small portion of the rim to start cutting first.

Buy a good-quality set of hole saws and you can use them for many different chores during the restoration of your car. Hole saws are available in sizes ranging from 5/8 inch to over 5 inches diameter in 1/8-inch increments. (See Sources of Supply—Lenox.)

WOODEN MALLETS AND DEAD-BLOW HAMMERS

A heavy hardwood mallet is as essential to woodworking as a ball-peen hammer is to mechanical work. I have a mallet made from hickory that is tough as nails and heavy enough to pack a wallop when assembling or disassembling joinery. This doesn't mean that I beat the heck out of the joinery, it simply means that the mallet has enough mass to persuade parts to move without a lot of violent hammering. Mass and inertia are wonderful allies when

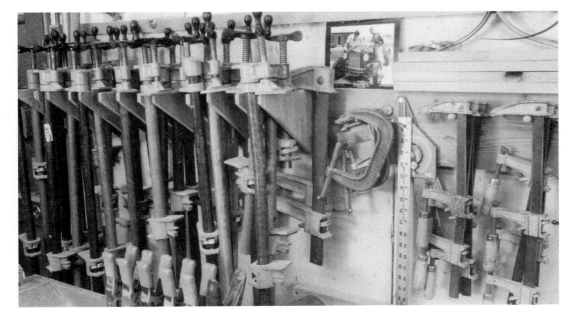

Clamps are essential to good woodworking. You can never have too many.

trying to get a tight-fitting joint together without damaging the wood.

Carving mallets are cylindrical in shape and are made from dense, heavy wood. The cylindrical shape helps keep the mallet's force centered on the end of the chisel. The point of impact of the mallet is directly through the center of the mallet, eliminating off-balance, glancing blows. I have several different-sized mallets for different purposes. A small mallet is good for delicate work, in which many light blows are needed to get the work done. The smaller mass lessens fatigue and increases operator control. My heavy mallets are for heavy wood removal. A sharp chisel and a heavy, well-balanced mallet can remove a lot of wood in a hurry. One thing to keep in mind is that when striking a chisel with the mallet, you should never lift the mallet more than 3 inches from the end of the handle. Any farther away, and the force is excessive and can damage the chisel handle, the work, or, if you miss the handle, your hand. There is no reason to need that much force unless your chisels are dull. I have watched a fellow break his hand by missing the chisel handle with a wild, impatient blow.

Dead-blow hammers are usually made from some type of plastic with lead or iron shot filling the hammer's head. This shot absorbs the rebound energy and deadens the blow, hence dead-blow. A dead-blow hammer is an effective tool for assembly and disassembly. Buy a good hammer made with nonmarring material.

CLAMPS

Pipe clamps come in two sizes, according to the pipe they fit, 1/2 inch and 3/4 inch in diameter. Pipe clamps fit on ordinary iron plumbing pipe. The head of the clamp screws to one end of the pipe and the foot of the clamp slides along the pipe automatically gripping the pipe at any point when pressure is applied to the foot. The foot locks in place by means of a set of quick-release cams or clutches.

Pipe clamps are the workhorses of a wood shop. Relatively inexpensive, pipe clamps can perform lots of clamping chores. Pipe comes in 10-foot lengths, but I cut it down to smaller sizes, as needed. If a person needs a really long clamp, you can join several lengths of pipe using pipe couplers. I often find myself needing clamps that exceed 8 feet in length, and the pipe clamp is the only show in town.

I use the 3/4-inch-diameter pipe clamps. Although they are heavier than the 1/2-inch clamps, I like the added leverage

Using a Spanish Windlass

A Spanish windlass is just a piece of nylon rope and a short stick. Loop the nylon rope around the object you want to clamp . . .

. . . and use the stick to twist the rope tight. You can exert a fair amount of pressure with a good rope.

and strength of the larger crank handle. For smaller, shorter clamps the, 1/2-inch pipe is a lot lighter and easier to handle.

Don't buy cheap pipe clamps. The clutches slip after a while and the threads on the head will usually bind as the pressure is increased. I use Jorgensen clamps, and they are built to last a lifetime.

Have a good pile of C-clamps or small sliding bar clamps on hand, too. You can never have too many clamps.

SHOP-MADE CLAMPS

Long before the days of hardware stores and mail-order outlets, woodworkers

relied on homemade clamps. A Spanish windlass, a length of rope, and a stick can handle many clamping chores. The rope is looped around the object to be clamped and a stick is inserted between the loops; the stick is then used to wind the rope and tighten it, just like a rubber band on a toy airplane. This clamping method is old as dirt and just as reliable. The trick is to use rope that doesn't stretch. Nylon rope will exert quite a bit of pressure when wound tight. This method is especially handy when clamping large frames, such as a quarter panel, when you don't have long enough clamps to reach.

Using a strongback and wedges is a good way to clamp panels. A strongback is simply a pair of boards that are fastened to a piece of plywood, another board, or a bench top. Space the boards a couple of inches farther apart than the material you are going to clamp. Cut some wedges out of scrap material, enough so you can use a pair of wedges every foot. Glue up your material, lay it between the strongbacks, and, using pairs of wedges, drive them tight between one strongback and the material being clamped. A tremendous amount of pressure can be exerted with the wedges, so make sure the strongbacks are securely mounted. You can quickly set up strongbacks for any width or length of material you are planning on laminating.

SCRAPERS AND SHAVE HOOKS

I use a 2-inch-wide **paint scraper** for cleaning dried glue off boards. Sharpen the scraper blade slightly convex and gently round the corners of the blade to prevent the tool from digging into the surface when used. A paint scraper can also remove a lot of wood but will leave a rough surface.

Cabinet scrapers are flat pieces of steel that have a burr along their edge. The burr acts like a tiny plane, taking shavings with each pass. Before sandpaper became readily available, cabinet scrapers were used to eliminate tool marks and scratches. I use my cabinet scrapers on figured wood because they won't cause tearout. They also work great for eliminating shear marks and other blemishes in veneer.

Cabinet scrapers are easy to use, but it takes some practice to learn how to raise the burr when you refresh the edge. Begin by filing the edge flat, then hone on a stone. Last, create the burr by rubbing the edge with a burnishing tool or the shank of a chisel held at a slight angle. A burr can be flattened and raised with the burnishing tool several times before the blade needs filing and honing.

Cabinet scrapers can be purchased with curved profiles for curved work. An old handsaw blade can be cut to create one. **Shave hooks** work like scrapers except they have a handle on them. A shave hook is sharpened to a knife-edge and not burnished. Shave hooks are great for cleaning out grooves and other molded surfaces when removing finish or paint. They aren't meant for finish work.

SHARPENING TOOLS

Obtaining a sharp edge on cutting tools is one of the most important skills a woodworker **must** learn. All the trick tools in the world are useless if they can't shear the fibers of the wood. Any cutting edge that is less than dead sharp will tear the fibers of the wood, rather than shear them, and tearing fibers requires a lot more effort than shearing them. Imagine the difference

This is a 2-inch paint scraper modified for scraping glue. The curved blade cleans the dried glue off the wood without gouging the surface.

A cabinet scraper can take very fine shavings, leaving the surface glass-smooth.

This is my sharpening equipment. From left are a diamond stone; a soft Arkansas stone, mounted in a wooden base; a slip stone; and below them, a piece of plate glass mounted in a wooden frame. I use the Super 77 spray adhesive for gluing sandpaper to the plate glass.

in effort between cutting a rope with a sharp knife versus a butter knife. Torn fibers also result in a rough surface and can cause the grain to split and tear-out.

Sharp tools are easy to achieve and maintain with good, basic sharpening equipment and an understanding of how to sharpen an edge. My sharpening equipment consists of a 3-by-8-inch 600-grit (medium) diamond stone, a 2-by-8-inch medium Arkansas stone, and a 12-by-24-inch piece of half-inch plate glass that I glue sandpaper to.

My usual sharpening procedure starts with the diamond stone if the tool is dull from normal use. The Arkansas stone is used for the final sharpening because it is a finer abrasive than the diamond stone and leaves the edge "scary sharp." If the tool is exceptionally dull or the edge has been damaged from being dropped or from contact with metal, I use the plate glass with sandpaper. Wet-or-dry and stearated sandpaper works the best, but virtually any abrasive paper will work. I start with 150-grit to do most of the work, then move up to 320, and then to the stones. You could do all of your sharpening on the glass by using 600 then 1,200-grit paper. Be sure to use a little water or

honing oil for lubrication. Arkansas stones need lubrication too. Always use honing oil on natural stones. Diamond stones can work dry, but I tend to use a little nonsilicone spray lube anyway, as it helps keep the stone clean.

The basic sharpening method is very simple. The first thing I do when I get a new chisel or plane is to lap the back of the cutter (cutter, blade, knife, chisel—I'll refer to them as the cutter in this section just for simplicity). A couple of passes over the diamond stone will show if the back of the cutter is flat. Hone it until it is absolutely flat. You don't have to lap the entire back, just the region extending 1 inch or so from the edge. Make sure you keep the cutter absolutely flat on the stone, or you will introduce a taper. When the back is flat, it is ready for the front or bevel edge to be sharpened. I grasp the cutter with both hands and stroke it across the stone. After a few strokes, I stop to check the contact pattern to make sure I am honing the cutter at the correct angle. It is easy to round the bevel by holding the cutter at too steep or shallow an angle or by rocking the cutter while honing. I continue to stroke the stone until I can feel a burr along the back side of the cutting edge.

This burr signifies that the cutter has been honed sharp. Turn the cutter over and with just a few strokes carefully hone the burr off the back. Turn back to the front side and with a few strokes hone the burr up again. Once more turn the cutter over and hone the burr off. This will usually leave a minuscule burr on the face side of the cutting edge that can be rolled off against a piece of leather or coarse cloth. This is known as stropping an edge. The easiest way to see if you have the cutter sharp is to try the edge on your thumbnail. Carefully push the sharp edge lightly along your nail raising the handle until the cutting edge bites into the nail. The lower the angle the sharper the cutter.

Practice sharpening until you can get a "scary sharp" edge every time you hit the stones. This is really important, and once you get the hang of it you will be amazed at how easy it is to get really good results and how little time it takes. I sharpen my tools constantly, because I know how much effort it really saves and how much better my workmanship is because of sharp cutters, knives, blades, and chisels.

If you have trouble keeping the correct angle while sharpening, there are a number of honing guides on the market that will keep the cutter at the correct angle as it passes over the stone. Experience will eventually give you the "feel" for the correct angle and then you can pitch the time-consuming guide.

POWER TOOLS

Good quality power tools, properly tuned, can save a lot of time and effort. Proper care of a power tool results in smooth, accurate, safe operation. Keep cutters, knives, and blades sharp. Keep tabletops and fences clean and slick (paste wax works well).

BELT SANDERS

Belt sanders are labeled by the size of the abrasive belt they use. The most common size is a 3x21-inch which has a 3-inch-wide

Sharpening a Chisel

With a soft Arkansas stone and honing oil, here I am honing the back of a chisel flat in preparation for sharpening.

In this picture, I am sharpening the bevel of the chisel. Notice how I am holding the chisel. I provide down force with my left hand while I provide the stroke with my right hand. My left hand also keeps the bevel flat on the stone.

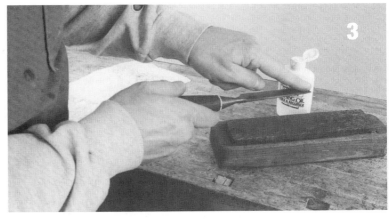

Feel the back edge of the blade for the burr that indicates the blade is sharp. Work the burr off on the stone or on a leather strap.

My 3x21-inch belt sander is a work-horse around the shop.

by 21-inch-long abrasive belt. The larger 3x24-inch and 4x24-inch belt sanders can remove more wood faster than a 3x21-inch, but I find the added size and weight make them clumsy and difficult to use for delicate work.

A portable belt sander is one of those tools that many woodworkers have a love/hate relationship with. A belt sander can remove a lot of wood in a hurry with a coarse-grit belt, and they can also do a lot of damage in a hurry, even with a fine belt. A little fine-tuning and some practice can help eliminate problems.

One of the most important items to tune up is the platen. The platen is the flat base between the sander's rollers. Quite often the platen is not flat. A quick fix is to remove the belt, the sheet metal cover, and any backing pad from the platen. Use a flat surface such as a table-saw top or jointer table, glue a piece of 150-grit sandpaper on it, and flatten the platen on the sander by sliding the sander back and forth on the paper. Just a few strokes and it will become evident if you have high spots on the platen. High spots are usually the cause of poor sanding performance as they will cause the sander to gouge the work. Sand the platen until it is completely flat, and you will have a belt sander that can sand flat.

I have a small belt sander that uses a 2-1/2x16-inch belt. It is called a Sand Cat and was made by Skil. It is a great tool for sanding and fitting small pieces and getting

A small belt sander is handy for jobs such as trimming off the end grain of this window frame. Here I am using a Skil Sand-Cat, a 2-1/2x16-inch belt sander.

into tight places. It is the power equivalent of the block plane. I don't believe they are made anymore, but if you can find a used one or a store than still has one in stock, buy it, as they are extremely handy.

FINISH SANDERS

Orbital sanders are the last power tools that should touch the wood before finish is applied. Finish sanders are designed to remove tiny imperfections, such as scratches, before the final hand sanding. A good finish sander should be light and have a dust pickup device of some kind. They create a lot of very fine dust.

Random-orbit sanders, also called dual-action (DA) sanders, do a good job of quickly removing blemishes but they can leave swirl marks if the operator isn't careful or moves the sander too fast. Sand slowly and finish sand with 150-grit discs, and you should end up with scratch-free wood.

ROUTERS

A router is the milling machine of woodworking tools. Rabbets, dadoes, tenons, shoulders, mortises—virtually all of the joinery procedures can be accomplished with a router. Fancy molding can

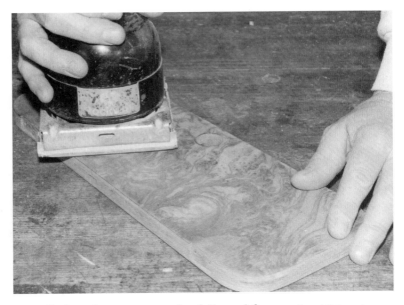

be milled, and patterns can be followed for accurate milling of intricate pieces. The router is probably one of the best tools around a woodie shop.

Buy a router that is at least 2 horsepower. For many jobs a 3 horsepower might be better, but the really powerful machines are large and heavy. Several manufacturers have recently come out with more compact 2- and 2-1/2-horsepower routers with alloy cases for lighter weight. These are the real deal and are incredibly handy.

An orbital sander can do a better finish sanding than a random-orbit sander, but will not remove material as fast. This makes it a better sander to use for delicate operations, such as sanding this veneered glove box door.

A random-orbit finish sander can remove wood in a hurry. The dust collector on the sander is a good feature to have on this dust maker.

My old "chrome-dome" router is great for light chores like rabbeting a frame. The new lightweight routers have more power than my old one, but for serious routing use a big router with at least 2-1/2 horsepower.

If your budget allows, get two routers. Buy one of the new lightweight routers for operations where you hand hold the tool and buy one of the big brutes for your router table. The big routers have the power to keep the bit speed high even during cuts that remove a lot of wood. Bit speed is important. When the bit starts to slow, it can create more heat because the feed rate has to slow accordingly. Heat burns wood and too slow a speed often causes tearout.

The router bit is held in place by the compression of the collet around the shaft of the bit. If the collet is not flexible enough, it may not keep the shaft from turning in the collet or moving out of the collet. The more flexible the collet the better, and slits in the collet make it flexible. I prefer a three-piece self-releasing collet. This style of collet has the most flexibility and does the best job of holding the bit, even if the bit's shaft is slightly undersized.

I use a dead man–style foot switch when routing. I often find that I need to stop a rabbet or dado, and a foot switch allows me to shut the tool off while keeping both hands on the machine until the bit stops spinning. Most router switches are located in positions where the operator doesn't necessarily have to let go of a handle to reach the switch, but often a

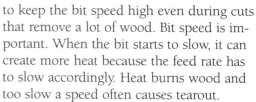

A router table is a great asset for cutting tenons and making moldings. My router table has a sturdy base, a homemade fence, and a hookup for dust collection. I also use a "dead man" foot switch, a great safety and convenience feature, to operate the router.

slight relaxing of one's grip on the handle is necessary to reach the switch. That can cause the router to move just enough to flaw the operation.

For a starter set of router bits buy these: 1/2-inch-, 3/8-inch-, and 1/4-inch-radius rounding over bits with bearing guides; 3/4-inch-, 1/2-inch-, 3/8-inch-, and 1/4-inch-diameter straight bits; a 45-degree chamfer bit, a long 3/4-inch-diameter straight bit with a bearing at the base of the bit for using as a flush cutter for patterns (see photo and Sources of Supply); and a small flush trim bit normally used for laminate trimming. This selection of bits will cover nearly all milling operation, short of larger profile moldings, that you will likely run into during construction of a body.

BISCUIT JOINERS

A relative newcomer to the world of woodworking, the biscuit joiner is wonderful for aligning boards during laminating. There are few things more frustrating than trying to get several boards flush with each other when gluing up wide stock. The glue is slippery and there always seems to be one board that just won't stay put as clamp pressure is applied.

A biscuit joiner cuts a 5-millimeter-thick slot in the edge or face of a board. To join parts, an elliptical "biscuit," made of compressed wood, is fitted into the slot. The biscuit aligns the pieces during assembly, and when exposed to glue it swells, helping to lock the joint.

CORDLESS DRILLS

A cordless drill is one of those truly great inventions. It is such a hassle to always be dragging a cord around, especially inside a car, where space is at a premium and you are often contorted into some bizarre position. I am especially fond of my right-angle drill. Not only is it cordless, but it is also compact, so it can reach those really awkward locations. Make sure you have an extra battery, so you aren't left

high and dry in the middle of an important operation.

JIGSAWS

The jigsaw is designed for cutting curves. The best jigsaws have a roller guide directly behind the blade. The guide keeps the blade perpendicular to the surface during the cut. This is an important feature, because without the guide a blade tends to wander and produce an angled cut.

The base of most jigsaws is adjustable for cutting at an angle. Higher-priced machines have a mechanism to adjust the up-and-down cutting action into an orbital pattern, which will cut more aggressively. I think that variable speed is essential, which allows you to control the cutting with more finesse.

It's important to have a variety of blades on hand. Wide, aggressive-toothed

Jigsaws are great for cutting curves. Note the angle of the jigsaw body during this compound-curve cut on a Model T seat frame.

My 18-inch band saw has 3 horsepower and can easily cut through 12-inch-thick hardwood. I use this saw for everything from resawing wide boards to scroll cutting.

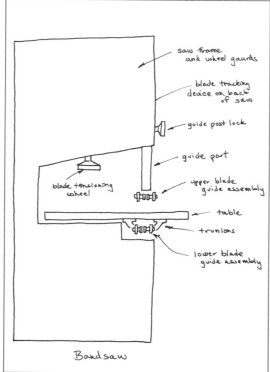

saw frame and wheel gaurds

blade tracking device on back of saw

guide post lock

guide post

upper blade guide assembly

blade tensioning wheel

table

trunions

lower blade guide assembly

Bandsaw

A band saw is one of the most versatile tools in the wood shop.

blades are great for rough work but won't be any good for fine work. A narrow, fine-toothed blade is needed for tight curves and clean cuts. With the correct blade a jigsaw will also cut ferrous and nonferrous metals; a drop or two of cutting oil may be necessary when cutting metal. The jigsaw is a versatile tool, and no woodshop is complete without one.

BAND SAWS

If I could only have one major power tool in my shop it would be a band saw.

The band saw is one of the most versatile tools in the woodworker's shop. The ability to rip wide and thick lumber with little waste, saw curves, bevels and cut joints makes it invaluable. In fact, the band saw is so important that I am going to detail what to look for in buying one and include a section on tune-up, maintenance, and proper use, something often lacking in manufacturers' manuals.

FEATURES TO LOOK FOR IN A BAND SAW

The best band saws have cast-iron frames, although a welded steel frame machine will work well if it is of good quality. Well-balanced wheels with hard rubber tires and good blade guides round out the necessities. Adequate horsepower will mean at least 1 horsepower if you plan to do any resawing. I own a 3-horsepower machine, and it can resaw an 8-inch-wide maple board with ease. Lower horsepower doesn't necessarily mean the saw won't cut thick wood, just that it will cut a lot slower. If impatience gets the best of the operator, a rushed cut will likely overheat the blade and destroy the cutting edge, resulting in a wandering cut and burned wood. Horsepower or patience, your choice. The upper guidepost should be stiff and not deflect under pressure. The table must be flat and should be supported by heavy trunions that move smoothly and can be locked securely for angle cutting. A positive stop for returning the table to 90 degrees will save a lot of time if you make frequent angle cuts.

An adjustable rip fence is necessary to be able to rip or resaw. A fence that is not adjustable is useless and should be relegated to the scrap heap. A homemade fence consisting of a heavy timber and a couple of big C-clamps will work as well as most store-bought fences. There are several fences on the market designed specifically for resawing and work quite well, but if money is tight, make your own fence.

Blade guides are critical to the operation of the saw. The guides don't have to be high-tech or high-dollar; they just have to be easy to adjust and not prone to shifting. The back guides, which support the back edge of the saw, are the most important. When a cut is started, the wood pushes the blade back against the guides. If the upper and lower guides are not in the same plane (both supporting the back of the blade), the blade is forced to twist, causing the cut to wander. I usually adjust my back guides so there is around five-thousandths of an inch between the blade and the guides when the saw is idling. That way the blade is not always riding on the bearing, which can cause premature bearing failure. Always be sure that the bearings are in good working order, spinning easily without any play. If the bearings stick, the blade will rub against them and cut grooves in the shoulder of the bearing, which will overheat the blade. You can always tell how well a band saw has been treated by the condition of the back guides.

The side blade guides keep the blade on course during the cut. Side blade guides take many forms with steel, wood, or phenolic (a type of plastic resin) blocks being the most common. Maple blocks soaked in kerosene have been used for over a century. The kerosene acts as a lubricant, and the wood can ride directly on the blade without causing problems. The only drawback is that modern saws have small guide block housings, and the small

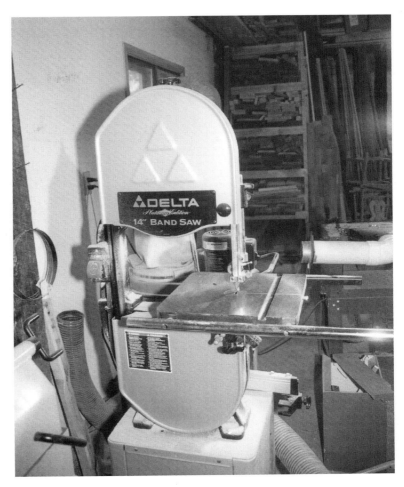

Delta's 14-inch band saw is one of the best on the market. Reasonable power, sturdy construction, and accurate guides make this saw a good choice.

surface area presented to the blade can cause excessive heat build-up if the guides are set too tight.

Metal guide blocks work, but not well. Set up properly, metal guides must not be in direct contact with the blade, and that "looseness" can cause a less than accurate cut. If the guides are fitted too tight to the blade, excessive heat and wear will quickly destroy a blade. If your saw has metal side guides, replace them with phenolic guides.

Phenolic guides can be set right against the blade. Also known by the trade name Cool Blocks, these phenolic blocks will not create excessive heat because they are slippery. If the teeth of the blade should accidentally happen to come in contact with the blocks, the teeth will not be dulled. When I use very narrow blades on my small band saw, I trap the blade in the middle of the guides for better stability. The guides will

47

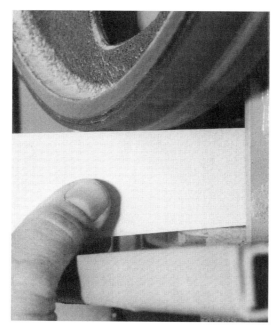

Look closely, and you can see the slight crown in the band saw's tire. This crown is essential to accurately tracking the blade.

show wear, but they can be restored by sanding or filing their faces smooth.

Bearing guides take a couple of different approaches. The European-style guide is currently the most popular on bigger band saws and has some definite advantages. If adjusted properly, the bearings will run against the blade, touching directly behind the gullets. This literally pinches the blade, forcing it to stay exactly on course.

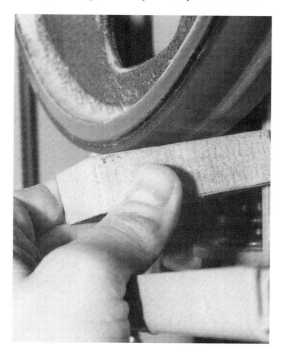

Sandpaper glued to a piece of hardwood makes a good tool for crowning flattened band saw tires. Only use hand power to turn the wheels while crowning the tires.

Side roller bearings operate in a similar fashion but with the full edge of the bearing running against the blade. These bearings are usually smaller than the European-style and can generate more heat in the blade. I have had people tell me that if the bearings don't touch the blade exactly opposite each other that the blade will be work-hardened by the minute flexing of the blade. Sounds like it could happen, but I have never seen it documented. The European-style guides work well if they are kept clean and rotating freely.

Band Saw Sizes

I wouldn't recommend anything smaller than a 14-inch bandsaw for a woodworking shop. A saw is sized by the diameter of the wheels, and this roughly equates to the maximum width of cut between the saw blade and the saw frame. Anything less than 14 inches can severely limit the saw's usefulness. There are many good cast-iron 14-inch band saws on the market for reasonable prices.

Height under the guides is another important consideration. If you are planning on resawing a lot of wide boards or need to cut compound curves in big pieces (such as the rear corner post on a woodie), you will need to have at least 8 inches under the guides. Most 14-inch saws can be fitted with an optional riser kit that will allow the saw to cut stock as wide as 12 inches.

Band Saw Tune-Up and Maintenance

Although basically a simple machine, a band saw has a number of parts that require proper adjustment and periodic tune-ups to perform at their best. I'll cover everything from the basics to refurbishing a worn machine. Once a band saw is tuned up, it will run smooth for many years with only minor adjustments required after changing blades.

The blade of a band saw runs on a wheel fitted with a rubber tire. Most band saw tires have a slight crown or hump, about 1/16 inch high, which helps keep

48

the blade tracking in the center of the wheel. Some band saw manufacturers run flat tires, no pun intended, and hang the teeth over the front of the tire. That's scary and of no particular advantage. I prefer the crowned tire approach. When you install a blade, center it on the crown.

Over time, the crown will wear down and flatten out. If you buy a used band saw and the crown is flat, the fix is easy. As long as there is a decent amount of rubber left on the tire, the crown can be reshaped with a 120-grit sanding block. For a sanding guide, I mark a centerline on the tire with chalk and then carefully sand from both sides to the line. Take your time and work carefully and don't remove too much rubber from the tire. And if the tires are worn, or you'd rather not bother reshaping them, replacements are available from the manufacturer.

Proper blade tension is necessary for a band saw to cut correctly. Most band saws have some device for determining the correct tension, but I prefer a more direct approach. With a blade installed, apply side pressure to the blade on the frame side using one finger and only one finger. As you push the blade you will notice that the blade deflects easily at first then suddenly stiffens. The distance between those two points should be about 1/4 inch for proper tension. I have used this method for years and my blades never break from over tensioning or wander due to insufficient tension A poorly tensioned blade will also create weird harmonic vibrations causing some real "interesting" saw patterns on the face of the cut. Decorative but not desired.

Once the blade is properly tensioned, its tracking must be adjusted. Spin the wheels by hand to see where the blade wants to settle on the tire. The upper wheel has a tracking adjustment, usually located on the back side of the machine, which simply tilts the wheel in or out. If your blade is tracking toward the front of the wheel the blade needs to be tilted back at the top, away from you if you are standing

Setting up a Band Saw

With the guides moved back and the upper wheel lowered, install the new blade. Using the tensioning device, raise the upper wheel, giving enough tension to the blade to allow proper tracking.

Spin the upper wheel by hand as you increase the tension on the blade. This will allow the blade to find its "track" on the tire.

49

Setting up a Band Saw continued.

The small knob in the center of the back cover is for tracking the blade. The knob tilts the upper wheel in or out to correct the tracking, centering the blade on the tire. A locking device keeps the knob from moving during sawing operations. The knob on the left locks the three-spoked wheel that raises and lowers the upper guidepost.

When the blade is properly tensioned, you should be able to push it about a quarter-inch to the side with moderate pressure. Too much tension causes excessive wear on the tires, and too little tension can cause sawing problems.

Adjust the side blade guides so that they sit just behind the gullets on the blade. Adjust the back bearing so that it is just a few thousandths of an inch (the thickness of a dollar bill) behind the blade. It is critical that both the upper and lower back bearings are exactly the same distance from the blade.

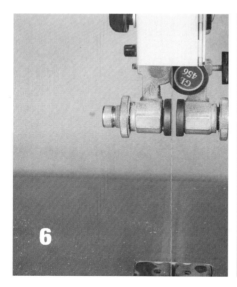

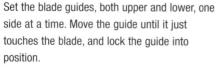

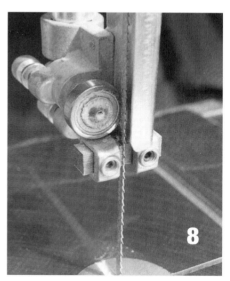

Set the blade guides, both upper and lower, one side at a time. Move the guide until it just touches the blade, and lock the guide into position.

Set the other side of the guides to match the first. Rotate the blade through the guides to make sure it is not pinched tight between the guides. With European-style blade guides such as these, the blade should be in light contact with the guides during operation.

Replacement guide blocks made of phenolic resin for saws such as the Delta can be set tight to the blade to provide very accurate blade support. The phenolic block is self-lubricating and will not create heat as it slides on the blade.

in front of the machine. The tracking adjustment mechanism pushes on the bearing carriage that holds the upper wheel. When you have the blade tracking in the middle of the wheel, make sure to tighten the locking device on the adjustment knob. Having the blade make a sudden tracking change is not fun. Once the train is running keep it on the track! Before you attempt a cut with the blade, run the saw for a minute or so with the covers closed then shut it down and check the location of the blade, which should be centered on (or close to) the crown. If you have to make a significant tracking adjustment, recheck the blade tension as the tilt of the upper wheel can increase or decrease tension.

Next the guides are adjusted. Improperly adjusted guides may adversely affect blade tracking and cause other problems. Adjusting the back bearings is critical to the accurate operation of the saw, especially when resawing. The back bearings have to be exactly the same distance behind the blade so that when pressure is applied to the blade, it will touch both upper and lower back bearings at the exact same time. If the blade touches one bearing first, it will be forced to twist slightly to touch the other bearing, resulting in a wandering cut. I usually leave a few thousandths of an inch clearance between the blade and the bearings. A dollar bill is a good "feeler gauge." With the back bearings accurately adjusted, I move on to the side guides.

I set the side guides one side at a time, both top and bottom. Move the guide until it slightly pushes against the blade. When you see the blade deflect just a bit, move the guide back until the blade is straight again. Do this a couple of times and you will see exactly where the blade and guide contact each other. Lock the guide securely and watch to see that it does not move while locking it. The European-style guides have a little play in them, so be sure to put enough pressure on the guide face that the play is taken up, otherwise the guides will not support the blade adequately.

A new band saw blade will run smoother if the back edges are smoothed. With the saw running, take a sharpening stone and carefully round off the square edges on the back of the blade. Be careful—too much pressure, and you can push the blade off the crown of the tires and derail the blade! The eased back edges will keep the blade from cutting grooves in the back bearing and are less likely to hang up in the cut if you need to back the blade up in the cut.

Every band saw blade, no matter what the quality, has its own lead angle or drift. This means that the blade will naturally cut slightly off to one side. This is not a problem if you are ripping or cutting to a scribed or drawn line, but if you are going to use the fence to rip or resaw, this drift must be taken into account. The easiest way to gauge and compensate for the drift is to use a piece of scrap wood about 3 feet long, jointed straight with a line scribed parallel to the jointed face. Start cutting the line and as you progress you will find that you have to push the board at a bit of an angle to stay on a straight line. Hold the board at this angle and shut the saw off. Carefully draw a line on the saw table along the edge of the board. Adjust the rip fence parallel to this angle. If you are using a board and clamps for a fence then set an adjustable T-bevel to that angle and reference off it when setting the shop-made fence. But before making a cut, test the setup with a piece of scrap. If your eyes are good, you will be able to see whether the teeth are centered in the kerf as the cut progresses.

Last, give the table a coat of nonsilicone wax and you ready to cut. Here are a few things to keep in mind when cutting:

- **Always** use a push stick for those last few inches of the cut.
- **Never** place your hand or fingers in the path of the blade when pushing the board. Sometime a soft spot in the wood will suddenly increase the feed rate dramatically,

and if your digits are in the way they will be removed. Band saws cut aggressively and quickly. Remember that band saws are the tool of choice for meat cutters!

- **Take** great care when backing out of a cut. It is easy to pull the blade off the crown of the tires, derailing the blade with serious consequences.
- **Never** cut so tight a radius that the blade twists. Use an appropriate-width blade for cutting the radius you want. (Narrower blades cut tighter radii.) A twisted blade will generate a lot of heat and can dull quickly or even break.
- **Always** keep the guides clean and working smoothly. They are essential to the quality of the cut.
- **Always** keep the work supported and in contact with the table immediately in front of the blade. This is especially important when cutting compound curves. (See chapter 4 for more about compound cuts.)

A good table saw is essential. This is my trusty 3-horsepower Delta Unisaw. Heavy construction, accurate adjustments, and a good fence create a good saw.

Band Saw Blades

A whole chapter could be devoted to band saw blades, but I will limit my treatise to a few specific types and some generalities on choosing the correct one. Blades are described by the number of teeth per inch, referred to as pitch, and by the style of tooth. There are two tooth shapes, regular and hook. Widths are available from a tiny 1/8 inch to a couple of inches.

A number of factors determine blade choice. Of primary importance is that there should always be at least three teeth engaged with the stock while cutting. If you are sawing 1-inch-thick stock, you would want a blade with a minimum pitch of 3 teeth per inch (tpi). When sawing thin stock, such as 1/4-inch paneling, the blade should be at least 12 tpi. The more teeth per inch, the smoother the cut. But extra teeth exert additional drag and will cut more slowly than a blade with fewer teeth. You would not want to try to resaw a 4-inch-wide board with a 12-pitch blade. It would take forever, and the blade would probably be ruined by the heat build-up.

Don't try to force a blade to cut a tighter radius than it is designed for. Any attempt to twist the blade will cause the cut to wander and produce a lot of friction, which generates heat and can quickly dull the teeth. If you have to force the blade to follow your line, the blade is too wide.

TABLE SAWS

The primary use of a table saw is to rip boards to width. The table saw can also be used to crosscut, miter, rabbet, and dado boards. Ripping a board, especially hardwood, requires a lot of power. I consider 1-1/2 horsepower to be the minimum power acceptable for a table saw. If a saw is underpowered, the speed of the blade will drop during the cut, causing the blade to heat up. When the blade heats up, the rim expands and the blade starts to warp. The warped blade will further burden the motor, causing the blade to rotate even slower, burning the edges of the board and creating a rough cut. The burned wood on the edge of a board will not take glue and must be removed. Sometimes the blade will simply jam in the cut and stall the motor. Adequate power will go a long way toward alleviating these problems. For automotive woodworking, choose a saw between 1-1/2 to 3 horsepower. Anything more is overkill. A sharp blade maximizes the power available and produces a clean cut. High-speed steel blades will work well as long as they are kept very sharp. If you don't mind frequent blade changes and sharpening, a steel blade will work well for any cutting need, but they are getting harder to find these days.

Carbide is better, but not all carbide is created equal. A good carbide blade will cost about twice the price of a cheap carbide blade but is worth every penny. It will be sharper right out of the box, and it will stay sharp longer and do a better job of cutting.

If you are looking for a used table saw, the old Sears table saws built in the 1950s and 1960s are good choices. With a little tuning, these saws will do a lot of good work for little money, even if you have to replace a burned-out motor. Old Delta and Rockwell contractor's saws are always a good bet. Avoid any saw that has a direct drive motor. If the motor dies, you will have to buy an expensive replacement instead of using a generic motor that uses a drive belt.

New, cheap table saws are not worth hauling home. The fences are usually abysmal, the motors are underpowered, and overall the machines are an exercise in frustration. They are usually incredibly noisy too. Let the weekend do-it-yourselfers suffer with that junk.

One of the quickest tune-ups you can perform on any table saw is to replace the original pulleys and belt. There are several kits on the market that consist of machined steel pulleys and a segmented belt.

I have installed these on several table saws and transformed them into smooth-running, vibration-free machines.

RADIAL ARM SAWS

The radial arm saw is a versatile piece of machinery. Perfect for cutting long lumber to length, the radial arm can also function as a shaper and a miter saw, and with a dado blade will cut decent tenons and lap joints. If you are careful and set the saw up with the antikickback pawls, it will do a good job of ripping boards.

Radial arm saws demand great respect. Because you are cutting over the wood and pulling the blade through the wood, the blade likes to pull itself into the wood (self feed) and jam in midcut. Special blades are required for safe, optimum radial arm saw performance. These have a negative hook. Always remember to feed the blade slowly into the wood.

Look for an old DeWalt if you want a really good radial arm saw. I have one that was built in 1958 and it is a great saw. It stays in adjustment even during heavy cutting, unlike some newer saws.

Never buy a cheap radial arm saw; they are worse than cheap table saws.

Dado Blade

A dado blade is used for cutting grooves, or dadoes, in wood. The dado

A good radial arm saw is quite versatile, although I use mine mainly for accurate crosscutting and cutting tenons with a dado blade.

Accurate laminations depend on boards with straight and square edges. A long-bed jointer will produce a straight, square edge with a minimum of effort.

blade consists of a pair of conventional-looking saw blades sandwiched around a set of chipper blades of various thicknesses. It is capable of cutting grooves from 1/4 inch wide to 7/8 inch wide in roughly 1/8-inch increments. A dado blade can be used on a table saw or radial arm saw and is ideal for cutting rabbets or removing the waste on tenons. (For more on using the dado blade, see chapter 4.)

POWER MITER BOXES

The power miter box is a handy tool to have for cutting boards to length and cutting miters. Not as versatile as a radial arm saw, it will still assure an accurate crosscut. Power miter boxes are available in two different styles. The original miter boxes were designed to cut simple miters from 0 to 90 degrees left or right of center and 90 degrees to the face of the board. Compound miter boxes also make cuts from 0 to 90 degrees left and right of center and will also make cuts from around 42 degrees to 90 degrees to the face of the board. This allows the saw to cut compound miters. Compound angled cuts are often used with wooden body framing and wooden bodies. Sliding compound miter boxes have the advantage of being able to cut wide boards.

JOINTER

The jointer is the power tool that replaced hand planes such as the Stanley Number 7. A jointer is designed to make a crooked board straight, both along one edge and on one face. A straight edge on a board is essential for good laminations and is hard to achieve with any other tool.

A jointer consists of an infeed table, a cutter head with three knives, and an outfeed table. The infeed table adjusts for depth of cut. If you are going to buy a jointer for your shop, make sure you buy one that has an adjustable outfeed table as this makes changing and resetting knives much easier.

Another thing to look at if you are buying a used tool is whether the tables are parallel. Use a long straightedge to see if the tables are parallel or if they sag, which isn't uncommon on old tools. A jointer with nonparallel tables won't give your wood a straight edge or flat face. Check to make sure the back fence is straight. I have seen a number of jointers that have a fence that has a twist in it. In fact I own one. The twist occurs from the cast-iron relaxing after it has been milled. There doesn't seem to be any permanent cure other than remachining the fence. Repairing some of these defects requires special skills or may cost more than the jointer, so stay away from machines with serious defects.

Operating a jointer is relatively easy, but there are some techniques that will assure accurately joined boards. Visually check the edge or face of the board you are about to join to find out where the wood will need to be removed to straighten the board. Start by removing the bulk of the waste first. When the board is close to being straight, start to make full-length passes across the jointer. Keep down pressure on the leading edge of the board on the infeed table as you start pushing the board past the cutter. Once the stock is started on the outfeed table, transfer the down pressure to the outfeed table for the rest of the cut. A little practice with some scrap lumber will give you a good idea of how to make a crooked board straight.

PORTABLE WORK BENCHES

A good workbench is as important as nearly any tool. Without a good way to hold the wood as you work, good joinery is nearly impossible and you run the risk of personal injury or damaging a project.

A big, heavy workbench with an end vise, bench dogs, and a pattern maker's vise is the ultimate, but many of us don't have the room for such a bench. A small, portable bench with good clamping abilities will work for the majority of the tasks used in building or rebuilding automotive wood parts.

I use a Black & Decker Workmate portable bench, which will clamp stock on edge, on end, and on its face, which covers almost any woodworking procedure. One of the best features of the bench is that it is portable, giving me the ability to set up a workstation near the car when fitting pieces of the body together. The bench also allows me to work outside the shop when space is limited and the project is physically large.

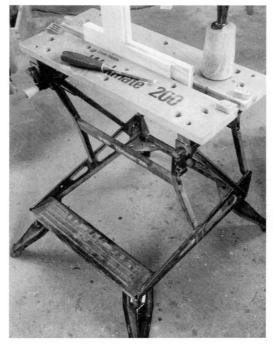

A portable workbench can assure accurate joinery by providing a sturdy work surface with good clamping ability.

The biggest drawback to the portable bench is its light weight. It is hard to keep the bench stationary when I am hand planing or doing other work that requires lots of physical power. There is a step built into the bench that allows a person to use his or her weight as an anchor, but it is often hard to do the work and be the weight at the same time. I have used quite a variety

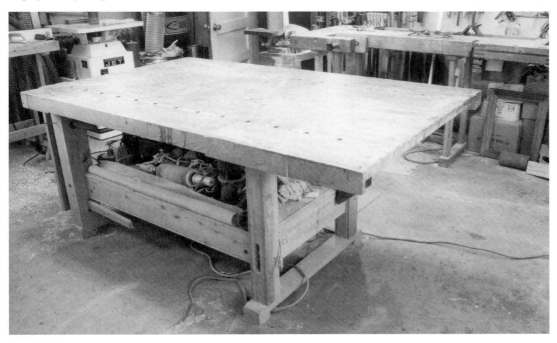

A good-sized, heavy, solid workbench is one of the best tools in the shop. In the background is my European-style joiner's bench.

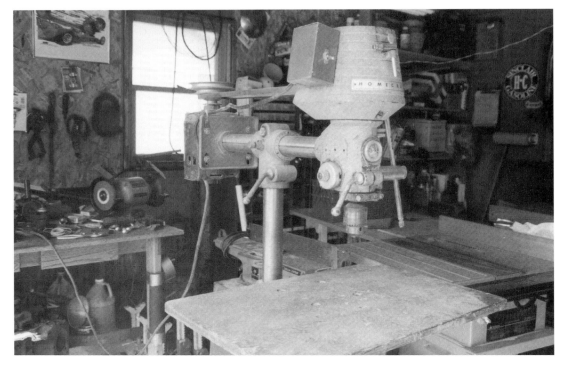

My radial drill press has the capacity to drill to the center of a 32-inch-diameter circle. The drill head will also swivel for boring holes at an angle. It is the ultimate wood shop drill press.

of ways to keep the bench from moving, including clamping the bench to a plank and then clamping the other end of the plank to a post in my shop. A 100-pound bag of sand draped across the step can also help keep the bench in place.

The addition of a hollow-chisel mortise attachment turns a drill press into a mortising machine. There are a variety of hollow chisel sizes available.

DRILL PRESSES

No shop should be without a drill press. Not only does it drill accurate holes, it can double as a spindle sander and a mortiser. Bench-top models will suffice for most of the operations in a wood shop. There are lots of good drill presses on the market. Make sure that a hollow-chisel mortising attachment is available for the drill press.

Hollow-Chisel Mortise Attachment

The most common joint used in building wooden bodies is the mortise and tenon. A quick, accurate way to cut a mortise is to use a hollow-chisel mortiser attached to a drill press. The attachment mounts on the quill of the drill press and holds a square chisel with a drill bit running through the middle of the chisel. The mortiser "drills" a square hole by removing the majority of the waste with the drill bit and shears the round hole into square with the chisel. Holes can be overlapped to provide a continuous mortise. This tool can save a lot of time when cutting mortises, and the mortise will always be square to the face of the board.

Joinery: The Art of Making Big Boards out of Little Boards

Joinery can be described as the process of fastening two boards together. A basic understanding of wood movement and grain orientation is essential for producing joinery that will withstand the moisture and temperature variations and the stress loads and vibration that a wooden car body is subjected to during its lifetime. Wood is constantly moving, and good joinery will compensate for that movement and keep things together.

Craftsmen have been joining boards together for centuries, and joinery techniques have changed little over that time span. With the advantage of good, modern tools

and modern glues, joinery is no longer the exclusive domain of woodworkers who have spent years learning their trade. The average woodworker can produce great joinery with a little practice and a basic understanding of how the joints work.

GLUE ALONE WON'T DO THE JOB

PVA glues (yellow glues) and isocyanate glues can provide a bond that is stronger than the surrounding wood, if the boards fit tightly together and the grain orientation is correct. Epoxy and urea resin glue will provide a stronger-than-wood bond even if the joinery is not tight. The best bonds, however, are mechanical, so

Edge-to-edge laminating is commonly used to create wide panels.

Two tactics for laminating wide planks: you can have all the grains curving the same direction (a), or flip-flop every other board (b).

that if the glue does fail for whatever reason (old glue, improper application, etc.) the parts will remain together. Structural joints such as mortise-and-tenon or dovetail joints do not rely solely on glue for their strength. Glue will make these joints tight and keep them from moving and flexing, but the joint itself will carry the load regardless of the presence of glue. If the glue fails, the joint will still remain intact.

LONG-GRAIN JOINTS

Glue bonds best to the long grain of wood. Long grain is just that, the long

fibers, which can be found on both faces and edges of a board. The ends of a board are short grain, which will absorb glue and starve the joint.

Any long-grain joint is strong when the boards are machined to fit tightly together.

Edge-to-face, face-to-face, and edge-to-edge joints are as strong as the surrounding wood.

Face-to-face, also known as stack laminate, is great for making thick boards out of thin. This is a great way to make stock thick enough for that windshield header when no material thick enough is available from the lumber dealer.

Boards are commonly glued edge-to-edge to create wide panels. An accurate joint with appropriate glue will produce a laminated wide board that is as strong as a natural wide board.

There are two theories on how to orient lumber when edge-gluing boards. Some recommend that all of the annual rings should face the same side up. This, in theory, allows a gentle, controllable cup in the board when the small boards move as a single unit. The other theory is to alternate (flip-flop) the rings, one board up, the next board down, and so on. That way

A face-to-edge joint creates a very strong "T" configuration.

End-grain to long-grain joints, also referred to as butt joints, will not hold with glue alone. Some mechanical means such as a tenon, biscuit, or dowel must be used to make the joint structurally sound.

the laminated panel will stay flatter overall because cupped boards will alternate. I use the flip-flop method for free-standing wide boards and the all-in-a-row theory for captured boards such as framed panels. Either way seems to work well; just be consistent. By the way, quarter-sawn lumber makes the most stable wide panels. If you are concerned about a wide panel cupping, use quarter-sawn lumber.

Face-to-edge joints are useful in automotive woodworking and can be used for making corner pieces. A face-to-edge joint also forms a "T," which can be very useful for increasing the strength of a rail or stile. These joints are basic and are relatively easy to do.

When stack laminating lumber, the annual rings in the lumber should all curve the same direction when viewed from the end of the board. This will keep all of the stresses moving in approximately the same direction. Don't combine flat sawn with quarter- or rift-sawn lumber, as they move differently and the stresses can cause glue-joint failure.

Remember that accurate machining with flat, tight-fitting surfaces will assure strong glue bonding and a strong joint. This is important.

END-GRAIN JOINTS

End-grain joints will not hold with glue. Mechanical means such as finger joints, a scarf joint, dowels, or dovetails are needed to hold an end-grain joint together. Finger joints were the manufacturer's choice when making long boards out of short boards and are evident in most woodie bodies. The joint looks like its name, a series of interlocking "fingers" that give the joint its strength. There are router and shaper bits available for producing finger joints, but I have never found any that produce the length of fingers that the original manufacturers used. The best bet is to avoid end-grain joints whenever possible.

BISCUIT JOINTS

The biscuit joint relies on thin, elliptical wafers of compressed wood for its strength. A special tool called, appropriately enough, a biscuit joiner, cuts a semicircular slot in the edge or face of a board. The compressed wafer is inserted into this slot along with glue. The glue swells the wafer, locking it into the slot.

Biscuit joints are excellent for aligning boards that are being laminated together. The biscuit assures quick, accurate alignment and

A dado joint is basically a groove cut in one board that will accept the end or edge of another board.

adds strength to the joint. Biscuit joining has basically replaced dowels as the alignment method of choice by most cabinetmakers.

Aside from panels, the biscuit joint does not have the strength needed for most other automotive applications. It can be useful in the shop for making jigs and fixtures that are always needed on any project. If a joint is relying on mechanical means for its strength, a biscuit or two can greatly ease assembly of the joint and will provide good shear strength.

BUTT JOINTS

The butt joint is the simplest of all woodworking joints. Simply butting one board to the other on the long-grain edge forms a butt joint. If your boards are accurately machined to fit tightly together, the glued butt joint is the strongest of all joints. The addition of dowels, biscuits, or splines can greatly ease alignment of the joint, but will not increase the strength of the joint.

A butt joint that consists of end grain to long grain is not a glueable joint and will need mechanical means to secure it. Dovetails, tenons, and dowels are mechanical means that will add strength to this type of butt joint. Screws will also work but will result in a joint that will move because of the limited shear surface of the screws.

DADOES

The dado joint is basically a groove cut in one board that will accept the end or edge of another board. This joint is a favorite of cabinetmakers for constructing case goods and shelving. The dado joint has a lot of shear strength and offers some glue surface for dadoed butt joints.

A through dado extends from edge to edge on a board. A stopped dado starts at one edge of a board and ends before reaching the other edge. A blind dado ends shy of either edge.

A dado can be cut with a dado blade on a table saw or radial arm saw. It can also be cut using a straight bit in a router or shaper.

DOVETAIL JOINERY

Dovetails are essentially wedge-shaped mortise-and-tenon joints, which give them mechanical strength. Dovetail joints consist of two parts: the tail, which is a tenon that is wider at its end than at its base, and a mortise, also referred to as a socket. The joint is extremely strong and resistant to separation from pulling apart.

There are primarily two styles of dovetail joint that will find use in a wood body or body frame, the through dovetail and the half-blind dovetail. The through dovetail has the tails and pins extending all the way through the board with the ends of both exposed. A half-blind dovetail keeps the end of the tail from being exposed by

The dovetail joint is one of the best ways of securing an end-grain joint. The tail locks securely in the socket, creating a very strong mechanical link.

These are the tools needed for cutting dovetail joints. Left to right are bench chisels, Dozuki saw, square, adjustable T-bevel, mallet, and clamps to hold the work piece while cutting the joint.

stopping the socket short of the edge of the board.

The dovetail joint is an effective means of locking end grain to cross grain without the need for mechanical devices such as screws or brackets. Dovetail joints have always been a favorite of cabinetmakers for holding drawers and case goods together. In automotive use the dovetail will usually be used as a single joint rather than a series of dovetails as you find in cabinets. A single dovetail can be cut on the end of floor cross-braces to lock them into the floor rails or to lock the cross-bows of a top to side rails.

Cutting a dovetail is relatively easy. The only tools necessary are a saw that cuts a narrow kerf, a sharp chisel, and a marking knife. I use a Dozuki saw for cutting my dovetails.

Any good-quality chisel will work for chopping the waste. Make sure it is razor sharp and sized appropriately to the size of the dovetail. A 1/4-inch-wide chisel won't work well for removing the waste on a 1-1/2-inch-wide dovetail. You need as wide a chisel as possible to get a straight, clean cut line on the sockets.

I usually start my dovetails by laying out the tails first. Some woodworkers prefer to lay out the sockets first. Personal preference, I guess. The results are the same either way. The angle of a dovetail is about 80 degrees. Any less and the tail might slip out of the socket; any more and the tips on the tails become fragile.

I cut down the sides of the tails, cutting to the waste side of the line and stopping the cut exactly at the base line. Accuracy is very important for a good fit. A good fit makes a strong joint. Next I take a razor knife and scribe the bottom of the waste between the tails. Use a straightedge to guide the knife and make very light cuts the first time across. Increase the depth of the cut by making several passes; this cut will be the stop cut for removing the waste with a chisel.

When the tails have been cut, use them as a template to lay out the sockets. I use the razor knife to scribe exactly along the sides of the tails onto the socket material. Be careful so you don't cut into the tails or you will get a poor-fitting joint. Again, scribe lightly at first and increase the depth of the cut once the line is established. This

Creating a dovetail joint

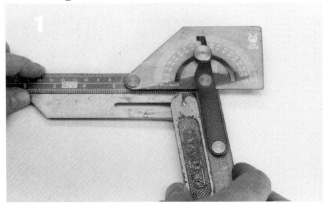

Use an adjustable T-bevel set to 80 degrees for laying out the dovetail.

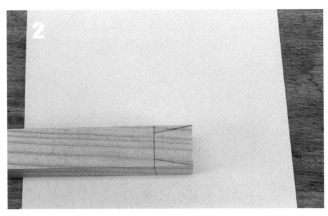

Mark the dovetail using a sharp pencil.

Using a band saw is a quick way to remove the waste. Use a fine-toothed blade, and cut to the waste side of the pencil line.

A sharp chisel cleans up the shoulder and side of the dovetail in short order. Be careful to keep the side of the tail square to the face.

Use a sharp knife to inscribe the outline of the dovetail on the socket board. A knife cut provides greater accuracy than a pencil line.

Carefully cut to the waste side of the inscribed line. The knife cut will provide a place for the saw cut to start. I prefer the thin kerf of a Dozuki saw to an American-style backsaw. The inscribed lines have been darkened with pencil to show up better on the photograph.

Use a sharp chisel to remove the waste from the socket.

I use my striking knife to remove a sliver of wood on the waste side of the scribe mark at the back of the socket. This will give me an accurate start for removing the remainder of the waste with a chisel. Do the same at the bottom of the socket.

Use a chisel to shear the sides of the socket clean and square to the face of the board. This operation will require a little shearing, a little waste removal, a little shearing, etc.

Remove the remainder of the waste from the back of the socket. Clean up the bottom, and the socket is done.

The finished socket is now ready for the tail.

Here's a nice tight fit. A little practice and all of your dovetails can turn out this well.

gradual depth cutting is very important when you are scribing end grain. It is devilishly hard to get a good scribe line at times because the knife has a tough time separating the end fibers for a nice sharp line. Be patient; you will get the hang of it with a couple of practice runs,. Use your saw to cut to the waste side of the scribed line and then, using the scribed lines cut the waste out of the socket with a bench chisel. If these are through dovetails, you can remove most of the waste with a dovetail saw and a coping saw.

If the resulting joint is tight, trim the offending material away with the bench chisel. If the joint is loose, thin pieces of wood or pieces of veneer can be used to shim the joint tight. You will find that making a usable dovetail joint is really pretty easy. Making a perfect dovetail joint, well, that's what practicing is all about.

DOWEL JOINTS

The dowel joint is not particularly strong unless you are using large dowels. Dowels are best used for alignment between

Use a doweling jig to drill the dowel holes. Make registration marks on the joint where the dowels will go. Notice that I have lettered the joint so it is easy to figure out which part fits with which at assembly time.

These dowels are inserted in one side of the joint and are ready for assembly. This joint is referred to as a doweled-butt joint.

boards and as a means of keeping boards from moving if a glue joint should fail.

Dowel joints are used for holding residential doors together but the dowels are large and the joint is usually aided by cope and stick joinery that adds considerable strength to the joint. Cope and stick joinery is the type of joint you see on paneled doors, where you have an ogee shape milled on the inside edge of the door framing and a mirror image relief cut into the end of rail where it meets the ogee on the stile.

I rarely use doweled joints since the rise in popularity of biscuit joints. Biscuits provide the same alignment abilities with slightly less structural strength. I use biscuits simply because they are an easy way to align boards during clamp-up, especially when a person is working alone with long stock.

I would suggest leaving dowels for the amateur woodworker and learn to use joinery that is structurally sound. The integrity of your car's body will benefit immensely.

DOWELED-BUTT JOINTS

The doweled-butt joint is only as strong as the dowels that hold it together. For example, if you are butt joining two 3-inch boards together with a couple of 3/8-inch dowels, the joint is only as strong as

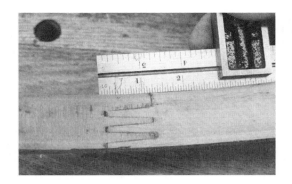

This is a finger joint from a Ford body. The fingers measure 1-3/16 inches in length . . .

. . . 1/4 inch at the base, and 1/8 inch at the tip.

the two 3/8-inch dowels, which isn't very strong at all.

A doweled-butt joint is fairly strong when shear is considered. If those same 3-inch boards were doweled butt to face with the anticipated pressure being shear pressure on the dowels, the joint would be reasonably strong, though not as strong as if the joint were a dado joint with the shear force being distributed along a shoulder the width of the board.

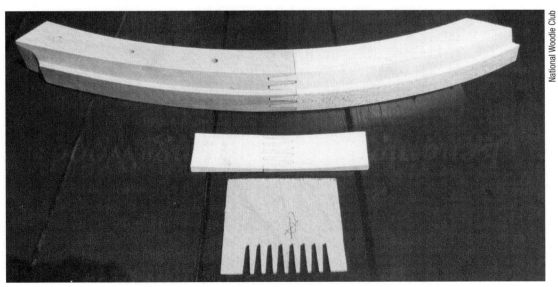

National Woodie Club

Make an accurate pattern for scribing the fingers on the timber. As with the dovetail joints, cut out one side of the finger joint first and use it to mark the matching joint.

A band saw works well for cutting the waste on a finger joint. Use an 1/8-inch chisel to clean the last bit of waste from the narrow end of the finger joint.

FINGER JOINTS

The finger joint consists of tapered fingers cut into the end of a board that interlock with the tapered fingers of another board creating a strong end-grain joint. The finger joint was a favorite of the old wood body manufacturers, as it was a way that boards could be joined to make long, thick curved pieces, especially wheelwell openings and quarter panel framing. Anyone who has spent any time with wooden cars will instantly recognize this joint.

Finger joints were originally cut with a shaper bit. It requires a big shaper and a large finger joint cutter to replicate the joints used on old bodies. The small finger joints that we see in millwork and flooring today do not have long enough fingers to

This picture shows the use of a custom cutter on a radial arm saw to cut finger joints.

give the strength needed for automotive use. A finger joint can be cut by hand, but it is tedious and exacting to make all the tapered fingers fit perfectly. If the restoration or construction needs finger joints for authenticity and you don't want to pop for the tooling, they will have to be hand cut.

Hand cutting a finger joint is similar in practice to cutting a dovetail. Lay out the fingers on one piece, saw down along the fingers, and chisel away at the base line to remove the waste. Use these fingers to lay out the matching fingers on the next piece. Practice and patience will result in a nicely fitting finger joint.

Parallel finger joints, also called box joints, can be milled on a table saw or by using a straight bit on a router table. Although they lack the visual appeal of the tapered joints, the parallel joints have almost as much strength as the tapered joint.

HALF-LAP JOINTS

A half-lap joint is one of the easiest ways to make long boards out of short boards or allow two boards to cross without needing to deal with butt joints. A half-lap joint consists of removing half the thickness of the lumber from two boards that overlap. The resulting joint is as thick as the original wood and forms a good glue surface.

A half-lap joint does not have good torsional strength because of the amount of end grain in the joint, but it does have good linear strength to keep the boards from pulling apart.

MORTISE-AND-TENON JOINTS

The mortise-and-tenon joint is the most commonly used method of joining wood in any woodie or wooden-framed body. A mortise and tenon joint consists of a mortise, which is a slot in the side or edge of a board, and a tenon, which is a projection formed on the end of a board. The tenon simply slips into the mortise, forming a strong joint with plenty of glue surface and shoulders around the tenon to

A custom jig holds the stock while the radial arm saw cuts the joints.

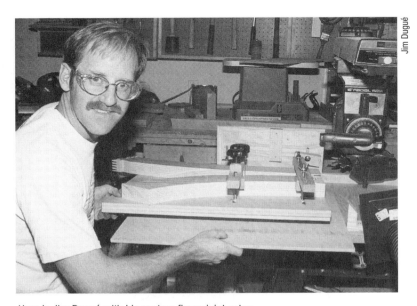

Here is Jim Dugué with his custom finger joint setup.

This is a half-lap joint used on a Model T seat frame.

keep torsional forces at bay. For added strength, the tenon can be pinned by inserting a dowel into a hole drilled through both the mortise-and-tenon. If the glue fails, the pin will hold the tenon in the mortise, maintaining the strength of the joint.

The mortise-and-tenon joint should be designed so that it has the maximum amount of long grain glue surface. In other words, the tenon should be made as long and wide as possible. A through tenon has a mortise that extends all the way through the board, allowing the tenon to do the same. A through tenon can be slotted with

wedges driven into the exposed end, locking the joint in place.

Mortise-and-tenon joints can also have the side of a tenon exposed. This is also known as a slip joint, because the tenon can slip sideways into the mortise.

Chop the mortise first. I use a mortise cutter attached to my drill press to cut fast, accurate mortises. A drill press with a regular drill bit or even a hand drill will remove most of the waste. Finish up by paring the walls of the mortise flat with a chisel. (See photos; also see chapter 3, the section on the hollow-chisel mortising attachment.)

To cut the waste on the tenon, I prefer to use a router table. A radial arm saw or table saw equipped with a dado blade will perform an adequate job of waste removal, but a router bit leaves a cleaner surface. A jig can be made for cutting the tenons on a table saw, but I always seem to find myself cutting boards that are longer than the distance between my table saw and the ceiling. A router table equipped with a straight bit will do a nice clean job of cutting a tenon and will leave a sharp shoulder without tearout.

I always make my tenons a very tight fit and use a small rabbet plane to trim

Here a half-lap joint is cut with a dado head blade on a radial arm saw.

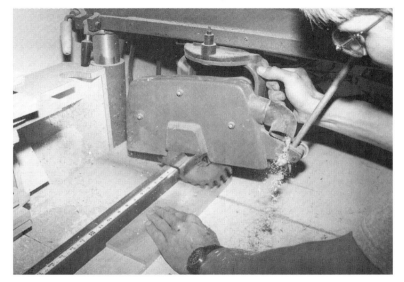

This is a rabbet-cutting bit for the router. Interchangeable bearings determine the backset of the rabbet.

them for a perfect fit. You don't want the tenons to fit overly tight or you run the risk of splitting the board when you insert the tenon into the mortise.

RABBETS

A rabbet is a groove cut into the edge of a board. Most of the use of rabbets in automotive woodworking will be for making inset panels. The easiest way to accomplish a rabbet on straight stock is to use a rabbet bit on a router table. If the stock is curved, a rabbet can be cut using a bearing-guided rabbet bit on a router and freehand cutting the rabbet. Care must be taken not to tip the router during the cut or the rabbet will have dished spots along its length.

SCARF JOINTS

The scarf joint can be used for joining two boards end to end. A simple scarf joint consists of long tapers cut on the end of each board, resulting in a long overlap of one board to the other. Because there is some end grain exposed, the scarf joint won't glue together with a lot of strength. It is a good joint for splicing in repair pieces that are not structural or that endure little stress. I would not recommend a simple scarf joint for joining wood for any framing.

There are more complex scarf joints that are structurally strong, but they are complex to cut and fit and are probably better left to the furniture makers.

This is a dado head blade on radial arm saw. The guard has been removed for the photo.

This photograph shows a scarf joint. Long tapers give a reasonably good glue surface, but it won't be as structurally sound as a direct face-to-face surface, like that found in a half-lap joint.

Creating a mortise-and-tenon joint

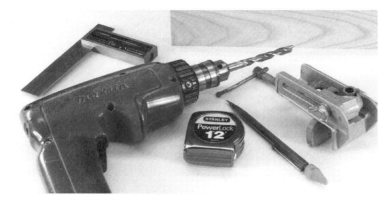

These are the basic tools needed for laying out and drilling a mortise with a doweling jig and hand drill.

Drill a series of overlapping holes using the doweling jig as a guide.

Overlapped holes need to be squared up with a chisel.

Overlapping holes can be drilled with a Forstner bit on a drill press. Clamp a fence to the drill press table to accurately center the holes on the edge of the board. The tape on the bit indicates when the bit reached the proper depth.

This is the finished mortise.

This mortise has been cut with a drill press–mounted mortising attachment.

Use an accurate square to lay out the tenons. I prefer to use a router to remove the waste from the tenon cheeks.

Set the router bit to the depth of the cheek and the fence to the length of the tenon.

Remove the waste with the router.

Reset the router for the removal of the waste on either edge of the tenon.

Test-fit the tenon to the mortise. If I am cutting only a couple of tenons, I usually make them a fuzz bigger than the mortise. If I am cutting lots of tenons, I take the extra time to set the router for cutting the exact tenon size.

Using a rabbet plane, I shave the fuzz off the tenon to provide an absolutely perfect fit.

Here is the finished product. Careful joinery will assure a strong joint that is capable of carrying tremendous loads.

Creating a Slip-Joint Tenon

A slip-joint tenon can be completely cut on saws. After laying out the mortise, I remove the majority of the waste with a fine blade on the band saw. Cut to the waste side of the layout line.

Trim close to the line with the band saw blade.

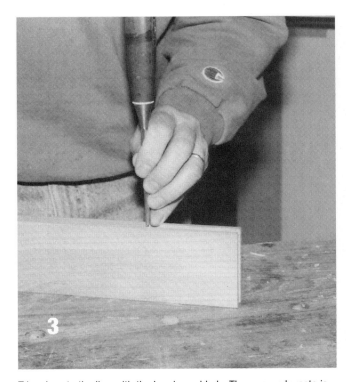

Trim close to the line with the band saw blade. The removed waste is on the left.

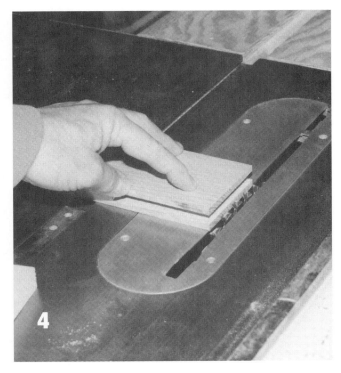

Use the mortise to set the table saw blade for cutting the cheeks. The table saw teeth should be set at the exact height of the mortise sides.

Creating a Slip-Joint Tenon *continued*

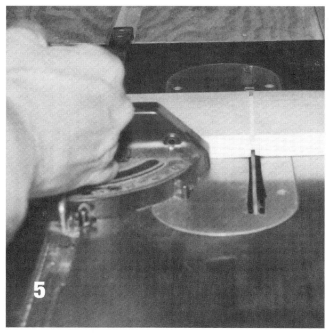

Make a pass over the saw blade on each side of the stock; this will be the square stop cut for removing the tenon cheeks.

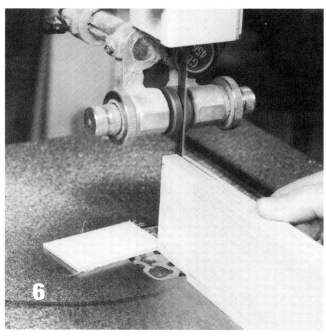

I use the band saw to remove the waste from the tenon cheeks. A dado blade or router table would work too.

Again, a bit of trimming with a rabbet plane assures a perfect fit.

The finished product, ready for glue-up. Notice how the joint "slips" together.

You can also cut a tenon by hand with a Dozuki saw. Split the layout lines with the saw kerf for an accurate tenon.

Cutting a Rabbet

The rabbet is cut along the edge of this frame for fitting a panel. Cut around the corner . . .

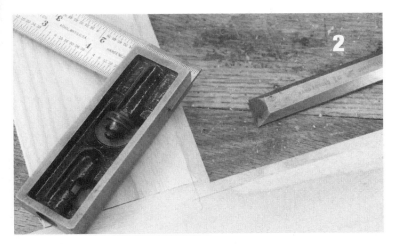

. . . draw the square corner . . .

It's a perfect fit, with the panel flush to the surface of the frame.

. . . and use a chisel to remove the waste, leaving a clean, square corner.

CHAPTER 5 FIVE

Bending and Shaping Wood

A short grain on a sawn curve can fracture under stress. Bent wood has a continuous grain, which eliminates this problem.

Shaping and bending wood are two quite different procedures. Shaping wood refers to modifying the shape of wood by removing material by various means such as sawing, sanding, or planing. Bending modifies the shape without removing wood.

If a project needs a curved piece of wood that does not need to provide structural support, such as an upholstery backer, the piece can simply be cut to shape regardless of grain orientation. The short woodgrain created when cutting a curve has little structural strength. But if a part demands structural support, bending

the wood is often the best solution. Bending wood, whether steam bent or laminate bent, will give the piece continuous grain and all the strength of a straight board.

Although there are literally hundreds of tools available for shaping wood, I am going to focus on tools the average woodworker may have in his or her shop. Just a few hand tools and one or two power tools can do anything that is required for shaping wood.

BUYING WOOD FOR BENDING

If the wood is to be steam bent, choose air-dried lumber with slightly

76

higher moisture content (usually around 15 percent). For more on moisture content of wood see chapter 2. If air-dried lumber can't be found, dehumidification-dried wood is the next best bet.

Unfortunately, most wood found at lumberyards today is dried in steam kilns. A steam kiln subjects the wood to a high temperature, usually around 170 degrees. Steam is injected into the kiln to help relieve the wood of stress, particularly case hardening, caused during the drying procedure. This is a quick way to get the moisture out of the wood but it seems to leave the wood structurally weaker than wood dried in other types of kilns. I have more breakage from steam-dried lumber than from all other types combined. But if that's all that's available, it might be a good idea to buy extra stock to account for breakage. Breakage, by the way, usually occurs during bending, so it will be immediately obvious.

The next important feature to look for is grain run-out. Grain run-out can cause splitting on the outside radius of the bend. Once the wood has split or fractured, it is nearly impossible to do an effective repair. Look for wood that has the longest continuous grain when viewed from the edge. This is equally important, whether the wood is to be steam bent or laminate bent.

BUILDING A BENDING FORM

Whether you use steam bending or laminate bending, a substantially constructed form will be needed. I construct most of the forms I use from medium density fiber-pine (MDF) or particleboard. Plywood and solid wood will work too but are usually more expensive. I have found a good source of form wood is the local cabinet shop. They have lots of plywood and MDF off-cuts that they are usually happy to get rid of. Steam bending forms need to be stronger than laminate bending forms because there will be more pressure exerted on the form during the bending process.

Landings for clamps must also be incorporated into the form. I use 3/4-inch

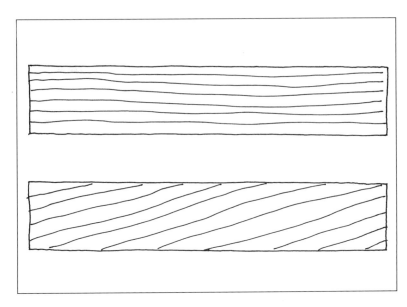

Jorgensen pipe clamps almost exclusively when I am steam-bending wood. The pipe clamps can exert a sufficient amount of pressure to bend the wood tight to the form. Clamping procedures vary, but I usually start clamping in the middle of a curve and progress outward from there. Build in many lands for clamps, especially when you are laminate bending where all of the laminates need to be pulled together along the entire length of the bend. Mount the form on a piece of plywood or some other backboard. This board will not only add strength to the form; it also makes it easy to keep the laminated board from slipping off the form during clamping.

A backer strip or two will help keep the outside woodgrain compressed and help minimize breakout of the grain on tight radius bends during steam or laminate bending. The backer strips should be the same width as the piece being bent, completely supporting the outside face and should be made of hardwood.

Keep in mind that it is much easier to bend wood around a convex form. Pulling wood into a concave form can be done but takes more power to pull the wood into the form as the entire curve has to be bent at once instead of incrementally as on a convex form. It is also harder to control breakout of the grain on a concave form.

This drawing shows the edge view of a board with straight grain (top) and one with grain run-out. Try to avoid grain run-out for steam bending, as the short grain can split during bending.

Here are the makings of a steam box, or in this case, a steam tube. Use Schedule 40 tubing for extra resistance to heat deformation. The steam box can be made to any size needed, simply by adding or subtracting lengths of tubing.

Drill a series of holes down the length of the tube and put wood doweling through the holes. This doweling will hold the wood in the middle of the tube for better steaming, and the doweling won't stain the wood.

STEAM BENDING

Steam bending is the process of bending wood that has been soaked in a bath of steam. Wood fibers are held together with natural glue called lignin, which comprises about 25 percent of the wood's composition. Heating wood with steam softens the lignin and allows the fibers to move or slide without damage when the wood is bent. When the wood fibers cool in their new position, they will again be bonded by the lignin and short of resteaming, the wood will retain the new shape permanently without any loss in strength. When I was a kid, I worked in a lumberyard where a "knot" of steam-bent ash adorned the office wall, a testament to the amazing flexibility of wood. Wood to be steam bent must be immersed in steam for approximately 45 minutes for each inch of board thickness. It's important to support the wood in the steamer (information on building a steamer follows) so that the stock is completely surrounded by steam. The width of the board has little effect on this time. Cool steam will require much longer steaming time, so keep the heat up and the steam flowing. A few times I have resorted to boiling the wood. This works, but it causes more raised grain and possible checking. Boiling wood is acceptable for hidden utility pieces but too rough for cosmetic wood.

A little practice with a few pieces of sacrificial wood will give you a good idea of the length of time needed in the steamer. Before you steam the wood, always make a dry run to make sure you have everything you need at hand, especially an adequate number of clamps. Steamed wood cools quickly; to take advantage of its flexibility you need to move fast. If you are working in a cold shop, heat the forms with a hair dryer just before you clamp the steamed wood to them. Warm forms give you just a little more time to clamp the bend.

BUILDING A STEAM BOX

I have a couple of steam boxes that I use around my shop. One is made from 3/4-inch plywood, lined with plastic, and has a hinged top. It is heavy and hard to store but is big enough to steam several pieces of wood at once. My other steam box is constructed from 4-inch PVC plastic pipe. The pipe and fittings are inexpensive, lightweight, and can be disassembled for easy storage.

The parts I used for the steam box's construction are a 10-foot length of 4-inch PVC, a 4x2x4-inch tee, and fittings to reduce the 2-inch outlet on the tee for a 3/4-inch hose barb. Cut the pipe and insert the tee in the middle for even steaming. You can make the pieces of pipe any length

you want, which is nice if you are steaming short pieces of wood. A smaller box requires less steam, and the whole process proceeds more quickly. This whole assembly can be friction fit together.

I use an old 8-quart pressure cooker to generate the steam. I have attached a copper pipe to the lid, combined with a hose barb that attaches to a length of 3/4 inch plastic tubing. The other end of the tubing attaches to the steam box. I use a Coleman stove to heat the water in the pressure cooker. If you use a pressure cooker, make sure the overpressure safety release in the lid is still functional.

Set the steam box on a couple of sawhorses and set the steamer up under the horses and box. The shorter distance the steam has to travel, the hotter it will be when it reaches the wood. Cheap and easy to assemble, this steam box has all the capacity needed for bending convertible top bows, steel body framing, and braces and brackets that a woodie body may need.

It's important to remember that steam can be dangerous when confined, so make

Everything's set and ready to steam. Make sure the steam can escape from the tube—trapped steam can be dangerous. I often stuff a rag in the open end to control the steam's flow. The rag can be pushed out by the steam if the pressure builds too high.

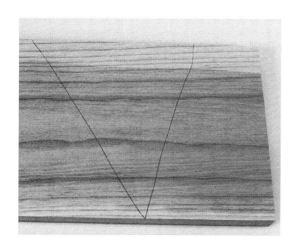

Before resawing a board into thin strips, mark a triangle on the board to make it easy to reassemble the strips in their original order.

sure there are adequate vents in your steaming apparatus to allow the steam to escape. I often just stuff a rag loosely in one end of the pipe, allowing the steam to escape past the rag. It is easy to adjust the rate of escaping steam and if the pressure builds, the rag will simply get pushed out, releasing the pressure.

LAMINATE BENDING

Bending a thin strip of wood is easier than bending a thick strip. Laminate bending uses this principle to bend wood without the need for steaming. For particularly tight bends, it may be necessary to steam bend laminated strips.

A band saw is the tool of choice for sawing a board into thin strips. A table saw will work if the wood is not too thick, but the relatively wide kerf left by the blade wastes precious wood. A band saw wastes half as much wood and can also cut thick planking or slice a wide board on edge for large laminated pieces. Before sawing the strips, mark a triangle across the edge of the board. This triangle will help realign the pieces when laminating so the grain will still have the proper orientation and appear to be of one piece rather than looking like plywood.

If the bend is particularly tight or if the wood available just won't bend without fracturing, the next step is to steam bend the laminates as a stack, without glue. Disassemble the stack after it has cooled and dried, apply glue to the pieces, and clamp to the form again. The steam will relax the wood enough that the thin

A band saw does the best job of sawing thin strips with very little waste.

Use the triangle to reassemble the strips in the correct order. This will keep the grain continuous and result in better-looking bent lamination.

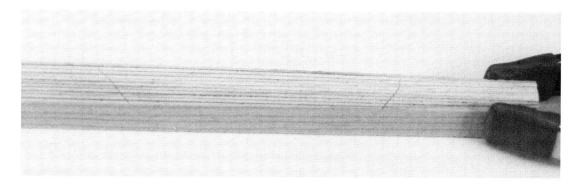

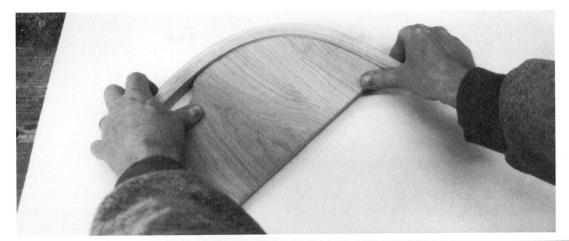

Laminations are easily bent around the form. Try this with a solid piece of wood!

A small short-nap paint roller works best for applying the glue to the laminate strips. Work quickly and don't exceed the open time of the glue.

Make sure you get an adequate amount of glue on the strips, keeping in mind that too much glue can cause a weak glue joint. A nice small bead of squeeze-out at clamping will show that the correct amount of glue is on the strip.

81

Laminating a Top Bow

Laminate bending a 1948 Oldsmobile top bow requires a larger form and long strips of wood. Urea resin glue is the best choice for a piece like this.

Lots of clamps are needed for a good glue bond.

Notice how the strips were cut overly long to make bending the sharp-end radius easier. The extra length makes a good lever.

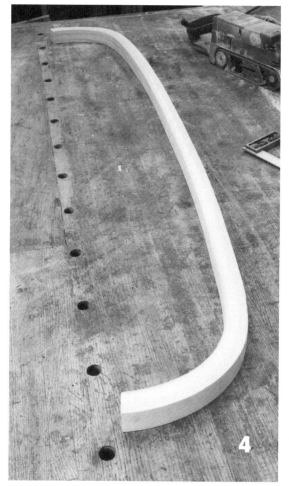

After removing the lamination from the form, sand or joint one side flat, then carefully rip to width on the table saw. The finished top bow is now ready for installation.

You will have virtually no spring-back with laminate bending, especially if thin laminations are used.

laminates should bend quite easily around even the most severe radius.

Laminate bending is also a good way to make a thick curved board out of thin boards. If your project requires a 2-inch-thick curved door post, it can easily be made from several thin boards sawn into strips. Careful matching of the grain will make the laminations almost invisible.

Glue is a big consideration with laminate bending. I try to use urea resin glue for all my laminate bending, but there are times when the tan glue line is too dark and I resort to using waterproof aliphatic resin glue. The reason for my preference of resin glue is that it won't creep the way aliphatic glue sometimes does. It is also completely waterproof and isn't affected by high heat.

HOLDING THE CURVE

Laminate bending is the hands-down champ when it comes to holding the same shape as the bending form. Steam-bent wood will not always keep the exact shape of the form it is being bent around. A phenomenon known as spring-back will occur when wood is released from the form. To match a specific radius, it is often necessary

Spring-back is evident with this steam-bent top bow. Experimentation is the best way to determine how much spring-back a certain curve will have.

Cutting a Compound Shape

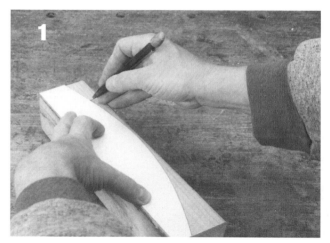

Trace the pattern on the piece of wood.

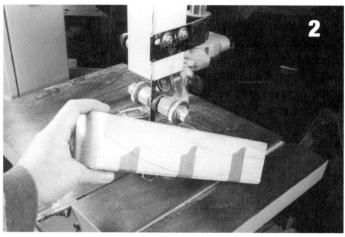

Make the first cut and tape the cut-off piece back on.

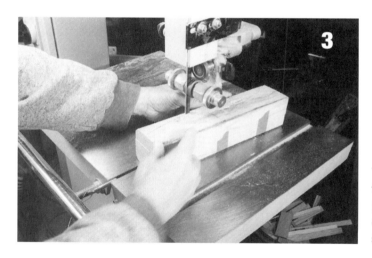

The tape holds the cut-off piece in place during the second cut.

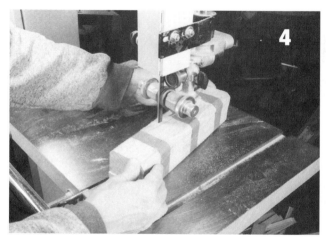

Tape the second piece back on and make the third cut.

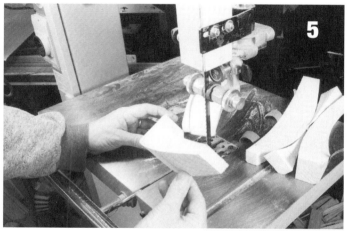

Remove the taped-on pieces and you have a perfect compound curve that was easy to cut.

to bend the wood to a tighter radius to accommodate the tension or spring-back. This is a bit of a black art, and the only way to solve the spring-back puzzle is to experiment. Keep in mind that it is better to make a bent piece larger than the finished piece needs to be. This extra size makes it possible to saw or shape the piece to the exact curve needed.

SHAPING AS A REDUCTION PROCESS

Shaping is literally removing any wood that does not match the desired shape. Various methods and tools can be used to make the work progress quickly and accurately. On flat stock I like to use patterns and a router with a pattern bit. If the piece has compound curves, saws, chisels, hand planes, rasps, grinders, and other highly abrasive tools are implemented.

SAWING

The first step in the shaping process is sawing. If the majority of the waste wood can be removed with a band saw, table saw, or scroll saw, considerable time can be saved.

The band saw is my favorite for shaping wood. Compound curves can be cut simply by cutting the piece on one plane, taping the scrap back on, and then cutting in the second plane or even the third plane if the piece is really complex.

If you don't have access to a band saw, a hand-held coping saw will do a good job, although slowly. A portable jigsaw is useful for relatively thin stock, but the blade is not adequately supported for sawing large timbers, such as a door pillar or rear corner posts. Even with a sharp blade and slow feed rate, it is very easy to accidentally force the blade to cut crooked. A reciprocating saw, also commonly referred to as a Sawzall, will remove wood quickly, although not necessarily accurately.

CHISEL AND GRIND

A body grinder, right angle grinder, or any number of other similar tools can be

Spokeshaves work well for removing wood from curved pieces.

used to remove waste wood. Open-coat abrasive discs do the best job, with 36-grit being my choice for fast removal. One big drawback of a grinder is the amount of dust it creates. There are more pleasant ways to remove the waste wood nearly as fast without the mess.

A good sharp wood chisel can remove a lot of wood. Care must be taken to make stop cuts to keep the grain from running out when removing large chunks of wood with a chisel. Gouges will remove a lot of wood from concave surfaces or inside of curves.

SPOKESHAVES GET CLOSE, QUICKLY

Once the majority of the waste wood is removed, spokeshaves are the best tools to quickly and accurately remove the remainder of the waste wood. Relatively cheap and easy to sharpen and adjust, a spokeshave can make a lot of wood disappear quickly with good control. A flat-face spokeshave is best suited for flat work and outside curves. The curved-face spokeshave is ideal for working the inside of curved pieces. In combination there are few surfaces that spokeshaves can't reach and do a good job of waste removal.

Buy a good spokeshave, Record is my preferred choice, and learn how to sharpen the cutter "scary sharp." (See chapter 2.)

Curved-sole spokeshaves work best on inside radius curves.

Flat-sole spokeshaves work on outside radius curves and flat surfaces. A well-tuned spokeshave can remove a lot of wood quickly.

BLOCK PLANES ARE HANDY

A well-tuned block plane can remove a lot of wood in a hurry, or it can take just whispers of wood off a compound-curved piece to get the shape just right. I always have my block plane handy when I am fitting pieces, especially curved work. (See chapter 2.)

SCRUB PLANES WORK WELL ON FLAT SURFACES.

Scrub planes have been used for centuries to remove large quantities of wood across the face of a board. Using a slightly convex cutter, a scrub plane can quickly take humps and bumps out of boards. I prefer to work diagonally to the grain, sighting down the board frequently to judge my progress. (See Chapter 2.)

RASPS AND FILES

I often find myself shaping odd curves and round shapes. I draw pencil lines along the wood representing lines that I want to shape to. A rasp will allow me to shape right to the line without worry of taking too much material or accidentally gouging the work. A half-round rasp is one of the handiest shaping tools in my kit. The flat side is great for shaping round pieces and the curved side is great for shaping inside curves. A four-in-hand rasp is literally four rasps in one and can remove a lot of wood in a hurry.

I have an assortment of rasps that I have accumulated from garage sales and flea markets. I have everything from a very coarse round rasp to very fine flat rasps and have found a use for them all.

Files get the shaping closer to the finished product. A good double-cut bastard file will leave a smooth finish while removing wood fairly fast. I have a tapered double-cut that I ground a smooth curve along the back to create a great detail file for cleaning up moldings and fairing body lines.

SANDING, THE FINAL FRONTIER

The final step in shaping is sanding. Once the waste wood has been eliminated, it is time to remove any tooling marks and lumps and bumps from the surfaces. Hand block sanders give you the most control. Power sanders can do a good job if a lot of wood still needs to be removed, but a block sander with the appropriate grit of sandpaper will offer more feel when working on compound curves. (For more on sanding, read the section entitled "Preparation of the Wood" in chapter 11.)

Making and Using Patterns

Patterns are an essential part of any craft. In woodworking, frame building, or upholstery work, patterns make the job easier and save materials from being wasted. Patterns can be easily changed and can be used to mock up assemblies or check out the fit of a piece. Life as a craftsman would be much harder without the use of good patterns.

PATTERN MATERIALS

The material you use for making a pattern depends on a number of things. Is the pattern going to be used more than once? Will it guide a tool or simply be used for tracing?

I make a lot of patterns out of posterboard. Cheap and readily available at hobby shops or office supply stores, posterboard can be cut with a scissors and is strong enough to endure some repeated use. Held together with masking tape, posterboard is strong enough to mock up assemblies, especially interior pieces.

Thin plywood will make a durable pattern. Although it is hard to get a good, crisp edge on thin plywood, it will still make good patterns for tracing rough cut parts.

Plastic, hardboard, plywood, and posterboard are ideal materials for making patterns. Here I have used posterboard to make a mirror-image pattern of a Model A interior support.

Making a Pattern from a Difficult Shape

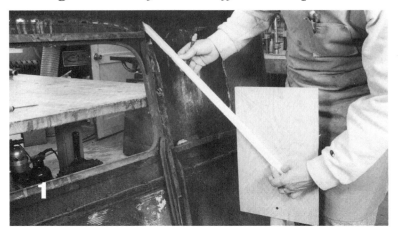

Using a pointed stick with a registration mark on it, touch the stick to the object to be patterned. Scribe a line on the plywood along the edge of the stick and make a mark on the plywood to record the location of the stick's registration mark.

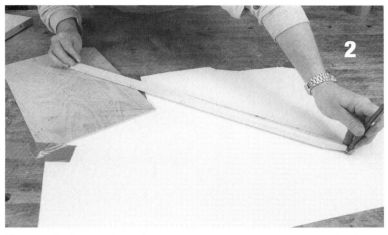

The more plot lines you have, the more accurate the pattern. Here I am using the stick to plot the points on a piece of posterboard.

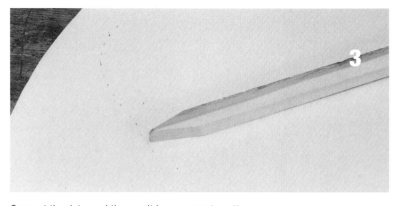

Connect the dots, and the result is an accurate pattern.

Plexiglas and Lexan make the best patterns. Durable and capable of finishing to a smooth, accurate outline, plastic is tough enough that patterns made from it will last through years of hard usage. I get my plastic from a friend who is a sign painter. Sign painters use lots of Plexiglas and Lexan and often have fairly good-sized scraps left over. They will be glad to get rid of the scraps as they are hard to dispose of in these days of environmental regulations. Old signs are another good source of plastic, although if the sign has been exposed to sunlight for a long time it may be a bit brittle.

Sheet metal will make very durable, permanent patterns. The drawback to using sheet metal is the time and effort involved, especially if there are lots of curves in the pattern. Sheet metal patterns can't be used with a router and pattern bit. A metal-cutting vertical band saw can greatly simplify making a metal pattern, but there will still be a lot of sanding and filing to get the edges smooth enough to use as a pattern. If you are looking for a pattern that will last a lifetime and won't break if you drop it, sheet metal is the material to use.

MAKING A PATTERN USING AN EXISTING PIECE

If you are fortunate enough to have usable pieces of original wood parts, use them to trace out patterns. Unless the piece is a simple, flat piece you will have to trace a face and a side pattern. If there are dings and dents or pieces missing in the original, draw them in on the pattern before cutting the pattern out.

MAKING A PATTERN FROM A DRAWING

If the drawing is to scale, there are a couple of ways to make a pattern from the drawing. The easiest method is to simply glue the drawing onto the pattern material with rubber cement and cut the pattern out. Once you have it cut out and the edges finished to the exact outline, simply

Using a profile gauge is a quick way to make a pattern of a curved or odd-shaped piece. I have made registration marks at every inch and will make corresponding patterns to follow the compound curve of the piece, an upper door rail from a 1950 Ford.

remove the paper drawing and you have an accurate pattern.

If you don't want to destroy the original drawing, have a copy made at your local copy shop and use it for the pattern. You can also use tracing paper and glue that to the pattern material or use good old-fashioned carbon paper and make a tracing of the pattern.

Tracing from a paper pattern is not always accurate. Sometimes it is difficult to trace the exact line and you end up with a pattern that is slightly different from the original. In most cases this won't be a problem, but if you are making a pattern that has to be exact, use a photocopy or the original drawing.

MAKING A PATTERN FROM A PICTURE

I have been faced with the task of making pieces with no more than a photo to go by. I start by enlarging the photo on a copier.

If you are having someone photograph a piece for you to use as a pattern, have them include a ruler in the photo so you can accurately get the piece to scale. If you have a photo of just the piece, try to get at

least one dimension so you have a basis to scale the photo from.

It is easy to make a scale to measure the dimensions from a picture or photograph. If you have one dimension, use that dimension and a drafting scale to make a scale to measure the other dimensions of the picture.

MAKING A PATTERN OF AN IRREGULAR SURFACE

There's a useful old trick that boat carpenters use for taking patterns off the inside of a hull when they are building partitions and cabinetry.

Start by making a stand or some device to hold a piece of thin plywood. Place the stand and plywood close to the surface to be patterned. Using a pointed stick with a registration mark on it, start plotting lines on the plywood by touching the point of the stick to the irregular surface, drawing a line along the stick on the plywood, and placing a mark on the plywood at the registration mark on the stick. Make a plot line as often as needed to get an accurate reading of the surface to be patterned. Once

Routing a Pattern

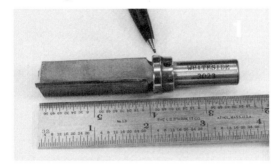

This is a pattern bit for use in a router. The pencil is pointing to the bearing that runs along the pattern. Use a high-horsepower router with this bit.

This is the pattern on top of the material to be trimmed. In this case I am making a bending form for a top bow.

The bit is installed in the router.

On large patterns I run the router over the pattern. Small parts I run over the router table for better stability and safety.

Here is the nearly finished form, an exact duplicate of the pattern.

you have all of the plot lines finished, re-move the plywood from the stand, lay it on a sheet of paper, plywood, plexiglass, etc., and reverse the procedure. Lay the stick on the plot lines, line up the registration mark, and make a dot at the point of the stick. When you have all of the points laid out, it is a simple matter of connecting the dots to get an accurate pattern of the irregular sur-face. The more complex the surface, the more plot lines, hence more dots, are need-ed. This is a neat trick and you will find lots of uses for it.

For small shapes that need to be copied, a profile gauge comes in handy. Profile gauges come in sizes from 6 to 18 inches long, and the best ones have plastic fingers. I use my profile gauge mostly for taking the profiles of moldings I need to duplicate, such as the beltline molding on woodies.

USING THE PATTERNS

The simplest way to use a pattern is to trace around it, then saw and shape the part to the lines. I take this method a step further and use the pattern with a router for final shaping. First I trace the pattern onto the piece of wood. I saw most of the waste material off the piece using a band saw, then I attach the pattern to the wood and use the pattern as a guide for the router bit to follow. Using a flush cut router bit with a guide bearing will pro-duce a part that is an exact duplicate of the pattern. So exact, in fact, that any tiny flaw in the pattern will be transferred to the finished piece. Make your patterns ac-curate, and you will have a nicely finished edge on your wood.

A pattern can be fastened to the wood by small brads or screws or by using carpet tape. Whatever method you use, make sure the pattern is secure. If the pattern shifts, it will ruin your piece and can even cause the router to cut too deeply and kick back. Us-ing a router is not only accurate, but it saves a lot of sanding and shaping. A sharp router bit will leave a finished surface that will not have to be sanded in most instances.

The best way to use a router and pat-tern is in a router table. That way you will be working over the bit and holding onto the pattern and wood. This method is much easier to control than running the router over the pattern and wood where you have the possibility of the router tip-ping off the edge of a narrow piece, and the added problem of securing the wood and pattern from moving.

If the piece is complex, such as a door post, several patterns will be needed with several cuts needed to reproduce the part.

If you have access to a shaper, it will do a better job than a router, although if the part has small, intricate details you will still have to use a router bit in the shaper. Shapers have more mass and are better able to dampen vibration while cutting, and they usually have more power than a router.

Fasteners, Brackets, and Hardware

For years the only wood screws used in woodies and wooden-framed bodies were raw steel, nickel-plated steel, or chrome-plated steel. Wood likes to hold moisture and that degrades the plating on such screws. As soon as the plating starts to degrade, rust appears and stains the surrounding wood. As the rust progresses it tends to hold more moisture, making a perfect environment for fungal growth. The combination of rust and fungus eliminates the holding power of the screw and results in joint failure. More than a few woodies met their end as they slowly dissolved into a pile of pieces because of rusting wood screws and rotting wood.

Stainless steel eliminates the rust problem. Screw holes still offer the potential for harboring fungus, but if stainless fasteners are used and bedded in epoxy when installed there is much less possibility of

wood degradation. Keep in mind that screws used inside a car are not immune to rust just because they are not directly exposed to rain. Humidity, especially in storage, can quickly rust plain steel screws.

There are times, especially during restoration work, where authenticity has to outweigh practicality and steel screws will have to be used. There are also the occasional specialty fasteners that are specific to a certain body or make of car and must be used to present an accurate restoration. A person can minimize the risk of rust by bedding these screws in epoxy. The epoxy will act as a moisture barrier and help the screws survive the moisture that is ever-present in wood. If you have a choice, choose stainless.

Always use wood screws. Drywall screws and sheet metal screws are designed for drywall and sheet metal, not wood. Wood screws are tapered so the entire screw grips the wood as it is driven. The taper also makes it easy to remove and reinstall wood screws without losing their ability to grip, and you will often find the need to dismantle and reassemble parts as the body is being built. Drywall screws tend to break more easily than wood screws, probably because they are hardened, making them less flexible. Drywall doesn't move around much after installation, at least we hope not, and cars move around a lot, or at least they are supposed to.

Here is a flathead stainless screw with a finish washer.

In my opinion, straight slot stainless steel wood screws are the only screws that should be used when fabricating a body or body framing out of wood. Straight slot screws are a bit more tedious to drive than Phillips head screws, but the slotted screw ultimately allows more torque to be applied to the screw, resulting in a stronger joint. Additionally, straight slot screws look more appropriate for a woodie body than Phillips head screws. Phillips head screws look better surrounded by metal.

Flat head screws are the most common style used during construction, because they will fit flush to the surface of the wood. Using a countersink to set the flat head screws flush accommodates a tight fit of overlapping pieces. Flat head screws will also disappear behind upholstery. Be sure to set the screws just flush with the surface. Setting the screws too deep will result in a dimple or depression if upholstered over. A tapered drill bit with a built-in countersink and depth stop makes installing flat head screws easy and accurate. (For more information on drill bits, see chapter 3.)

Oval head screws, especially when used with a stainless steel finish washer, provide nice-looking finish screws for use on door panels and other places where the screws are visible. Flat head and oval head stainless steel screws and finish washers are available from specialty suppliers such as Jamestown Distributors. (See Sources of Supply.)

Be sure to lubricate the screws before installing them. Beeswax or candle wax will do a good job of providing lubrication to help the screw threads slip through the wood fibers. Don't use soap, especially if you are using unplated screws. Soap is corrosive and will damage steel screws.

If you are bedding your screws in epoxy, run the waxed screw into the hole first then back the screw out, coat the screw threads with epoxy, and reinstall. The epoxy won't bond to the wax but the reason for the epoxy isn't to hold the screw

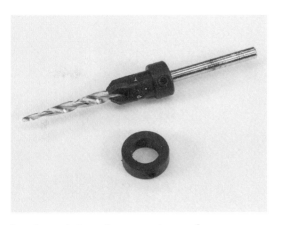

This tapered drill bit has a removable countersink. A stop collar can be added to ensure accurate depth of the countersink. The set is available in a number of sizes corresponding to screw sizes.

in place, it is to keep moisture from penetrating the screw hole around the screw.

NAILS

Body nails were commonly used in early wooden-framed metal bodies. Body nails were different from ordinary carpentry nails in that they had oval heads, making them easier to drive tight without hitting the sheet metal. Body nails also rusted easily and were responsible for lots of loose sheet metal in early bodies.

There is really no use for nails in a wooden car body. Nails are not designed to hold a moving, twisting body together. The only use for a nail would be to hold parts together while glue dries, and screws are a better choice. Screws hold the pieces together even if the glue fails. Screws can be easily removed and replaced for repair work or during construction.

This shows stainless steel wood screws and finish washers being installed on a door panel. Wax the screw threads to ease installation.

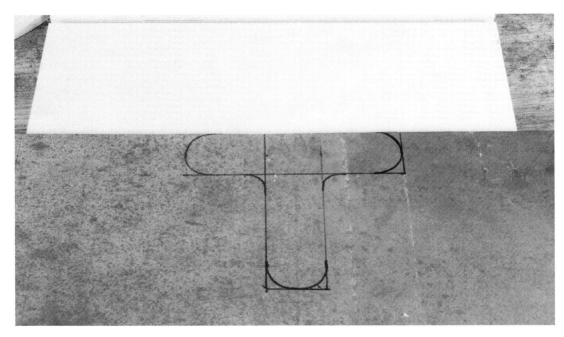

This is the pattern for an interior bracket laid out on 19-gauge mild steel. Drill holes for the tight inside radii.

The only place nails are appropriate is for fabric top installation. Small nails, usually tacks, hold the rain gutters, trim moldings, and Hydem Welt in place. There is little stress placed on these tacks because there are a lot of them spaced close together. Buy plated tacks and as long as they are adequately protected from getting wet, they will perform their task admirably for many years. Plated tacks are available from LeBaron Bonney Co. (See Sources of Supply.)

BRACKETS

If you are building a body from scratch, you will need to fabricate a number of brackets. The brackets will be used to reinforce areas such as the door posts, both at the base and at the top; rear corners; tailgates; the joint where the header meets the windshield assembly; and various other places as needed to give support to wood framing.

There are sources for early Ford–style brackets, and these could possibly be used for a custom body. If you are building a Model A–style woodie or a Model T–style depot hack, there are reproduction brackets available for these cars. (See Sources of Supply.)

Later-model woodies usually had complex brackets, many of which were cast. To my knowledge, no one is reproducing these brackets so you will either have to scrounge the antique parts dealers and swap meets for used parts or fabricate new ones. It is possible to have new brackets cast, if you can find someone willing to loan you a pattern bracket and you know of a good foundry willing to do small items.

Noncast brackets may be fabricated from steel or aluminum. Steel is stronger, so thinner material can be used. Steel can also be powder-coated to prevent rusting. Welding steel is easy using an oxyacetylene torch or an arc welder. Aluminum is easier to machine but is a bit harder to weld. Specialized welding equipment or a real talent with a torch is needed to do a good job of welding aluminum.

Steel and aluminum can be plated. Steel can be nickel or chromeplated by most plating shops for a reasonable price, especially if you have the bracket already sanded and polished. Aluminum requires the use of arsenic in the plating process, and most small plating shops can't use arsenic because of hazardous chemical laws. Aluminum will be more costly to plate but can be polished and lacquered as an alternative to plating, or it can be bead blasted and used as-is.

Aluminum or steel can be easily cut using a jigsaw with a metal-cutting blade. Use the slowest speed on the jigsaw and use a good cutting oil to keep things cool and keep the aluminum from sticking to the blade's teeth. There are a number of blades available for cutting metal; check with the manufacturer for the appropriate blade for steel or aluminum. A reciprocating saw, although a bit unwieldy, can also be used to cut brackets, although tight radius cuts won't be possible because narrow blades aren't available. If you are fortunate enough to have a metal-cutting band saw in your shop, bracket making will be easy.

Make posterboard patterns of the brackets before you start cutting metal. It's a lot easier to cut and fit posterboard than to cut and fit the metal pieces, and it speeds up the whole process considerably. Remember that the brackets will be mirror image from one side of the body to the other, so patterns can be disassembled and reversed for the brackets on the opposite side of the body. Make sure the patterns fit tightly and make them nice looking by radiusing corners.

Countersink all of the drilled holes and use either flat head or oval head screws to give the brackets a nice clean look. Remember that most of these brackets will be exposed in the finished car, so make them as finished as possible.

HINGES

Piano-type hinges are often used for flat doors. Early woodies had flat doors, and where the cowl curved in toward the frame, the wooden body was simply squared off for a flat post with the gap between the cowl and the post filled with wood. This was a practical, if not exactly elegant, solution.

As cars became more curvaceous, regular automotive door hinges were used. These hinges have varying lengths so the hinge pins remain on a straight axis from one hinge to the next. A major drawback

Use lubricant and slow blade speed while cutting the bracket with a metal-cutting blade in a jigsaw.

to these hinges is the small surface area where the hinge meets the wood. Usually only three or four screws hold the hinge to the door. Even with the hinge mortised into the door frame the attachment area is not enough and doors often came loose or sagged. A piano hinge has lots of screws supporting the door over a large area and does a great job of holding a door. Doors take a lot of abuse not only from opening and closing but also from supporting the weight of the door as the car bounces and vibrates down the road.

If you have flat posts and doors, use piano hinges. Commercial hinges are available from good hardware dealers and can be purchased in unpainted raw steel or stainless steel. Buy the stainless and solve the rust problem typical of plain steel hinges. That rust will leave black stains on the wood. Avoid the small, light-weight piano hinges found at most lumberyards and building centers because they won't be able to carry the weight of a woodie door. (See Sources of Supply for stainless hinge dealers.)

Hinges for curved doors can be fabricated or hinges from a steel body can be used. If you use regular hinges, make sure the mortises fit perfectly tight and use the largest, longest screws possible. Bed the hinges in epoxy when you do the final installation of the door and check the screws frequently to make sure they stay tight.

BEDDING HARDWARE IN EPOXY

One problem I have noticed on many old woodies is that rot almost always starts behind hardware such as door latches, trim, and hinges. Water becomes trapped behind these tight-fitting pieces and quickly ruins the finish. Once the finish is gone or degraded, water soaks into the wood and keeps the wood damp enough for fungus to start eating the wood. One way to stop or at least slow this process is to bed the hardware in epoxy when the hardware is installed. The epoxy binds to the finish or wood and to the hardware making a watertight seal that is extremely resistant to vibration and temperature changes.

Before bedding the hardware in epoxy, do a dry run of the hardware installation to make sure everything fits and the assembly procedure is efficient. After the fit is determined, apply the epoxy to the hardware and fasten the hardware in place. Excess squeeze-out can be cleaned up with a lacquer thinner if the finish is resistant to it. If lacquer thinner dissolves the finish, soap and warm water will do a reasonable job of removing the excess epoxy if it is cleaned up immediately after application.

Installing trim using epoxy is a bit trickier. Before installing the trim take a cotton swab or a small paintbrush and cover the inside of the attachment hole with a coat of epoxy. When the trim is installed, cover the bolt or screw with epoxy to help seal the attachment hole. Make sure to wipe the bolt threads clean on the backside before installing the nut or it may be nearly impossible to remove the nut sometime in the future. If you are using blind nuts, make sure the epoxy doesn't get into the nut, only on the shaft and the back of the head.

Use a slow-set epoxy such as System Three's T-88. (See Sources of Supply.) A good quality epoxy does not get brittle with age and will stay adhered to the hardware and wood for a long time. Good quality epoxies are usually slow setting, so be sure the pieces are allowed to cure out before being subjected to movement or stress.

Color Gallery

Wood Samples

White ash is one of the best woods
for making car bodies and body frames.

Cherry is a beautiful wood that has long been prized
by furniture makers and would make wonderful interior trim.

Ribbon-striped African mahogany
is one of the nicest paneling woods available.

Honduras mahogany is another prized furniture wood
that could make beautiful interior trim, or an entire body.

Maple, highly regarded as a good woodie wood,
was used on many production woodies.
Maple's light color offers nice contrast to mahogany paneling.

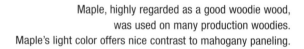

Interior trim made from walnut
would have the elegance of fine furniture.

Walnut burl has been used for decades by
British and European auto manufacturers for dash and interior trim.
Walnut burl has a dark brown color and incredible grain patterns
that add warmth and elegance to any interior.

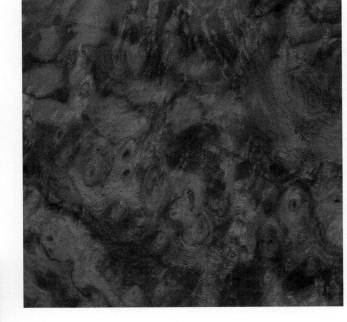

Carpathian elm burl, one of the most beautiful burls in the world,
has been used to cover the interior trim of many vintage luxury cars.
A woodie body with Carpathian elm paneling would be
absolutely electrifying.

Bird's-eye maple occasionally shows up
on vintage woodies. A woodie constructed entirely of
bird's-eye framing would be wild.

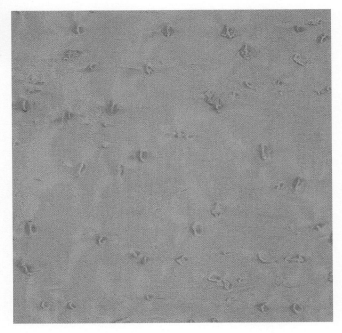

Curly maple is another wood that occasionally
shows up on vintage and new woodies.
Curly maple seems to shimmer when sunlight plays across it.

Pomelle sapele has a perceived texture
because of the grain configuration. This would make
an outstanding paneling wood for interior or exterior use.

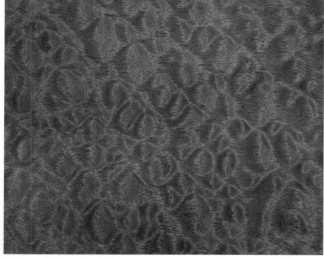

Lacewood has a beautifully uniform small-flake pattern
that resembles lace. Lacewood's light color and consistent grain
pattern make it an ideal veneer for light-colored interior woodwork
and would be outstanding as a panel veneer on a woodie.

A true rosewood, (*Dalbergia latifolia*), Indian Rosewood has a beautifully complex grain pattern with coloring that can range from golden brown to dark violet or purple with black streaking. As the wood acquires a patina from exposure to the sun, the violet will turn to a deep reddish brown. This is a fine choice for an elegant interior veneer.

Another true rosewood, (*Dalbergia Nigra*), Brazilian Rosewood has been a prized furniture veneer for more than a century. Recent bans on the exportation of rosewood from Brazil have led to a scarcity of top-grade veneer, but a little searching of veneer dealers can usually turn up suitable veneer.
Top-grade veneer will be deep reddish brown with black streaking and incredibly beautiful grain patterns. Expect narrow widths and lighter color on veneer that is currently available.
Brazilian Rosewood is one of the most beautiful woods in the world!

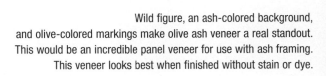

Wild figure, an ash-colored background, and olive-colored markings make olive ash veneer a real standout. This would be an incredible panel veneer for use with ash framing. This veneer looks best when finished without stain or dye.

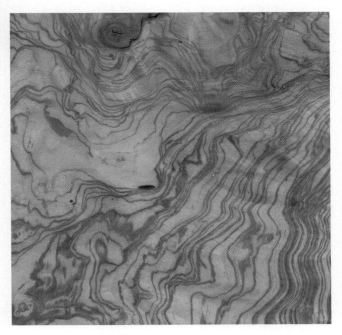

Applying Finish

Before the first coat of finish is applied, be sure to thoroughly clean the bare wood. Use clean compressed air and a tack cloth to remove all traces of sanding residue, especially in tight corners and recesses.

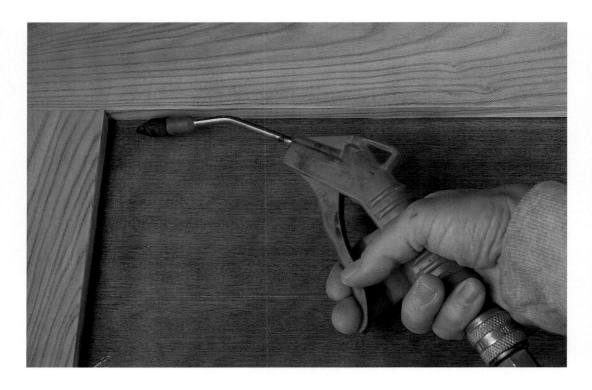

A good-quality foam brush works well for applying varnish, especially in tight corners. Apply enough finish to cover the surface but not so much that it pools or runs.

After the finish has thoroughly dried, use a nonfilling sandpaper to sand it smooth. Note the glossy low spots caused by the woodgrain.

This is how the first coats will look after sanding. The wood "grain" is lower than the surrounding wood; it will remain glossy each time the wood is sanded, until the finish fills the grain to the same level as the surrounding wood.

After a number of coats of varnish, sanded between each coat, the wood-grain is filled and ready for the final varnish. The surface should be dead flat with no glossy grain marks for a top-quality "mirror finish." Here I am tacking the surface in preparation for the final coat.

A high-gloss, grain-filled "bright" finish is beautiful to look at and easy to maintain. Note the reflection of the can in the finish of the wood panel.

Examples from Wooden-Bodied Cars

Before starting a woodie project, it is a good idea to obtain as much reference material as you can find. My collection has been years in the making and is a wealth of information.

This 1950 Ford is well on its way to receiving a new wooden skin. The later model woodies used wood more as decoration than as structural support. A fresh paint job on a steel body made this wood restoration a lot more time- consuming and expensive.

Doug and Suzy Carr

Buying plywood sheets with identical veneers will result in continuous, matching grain from panel to panel. The woodgrain on this car appears to be one board from front-to-back and top to bottom. The quality of the grain match in the panels can make or break a good restoration.

A hot rod woodie may be your heart's desire. Custom or "phantom" woodies usually utilize a stock cowl and fenders. This 1934 Ford has a stock-style body that covers modern mechanicals.

This is a stock 1934 Ford body. Notice the additional stiles in the doors and quarter panels, which differentiate it from a custom body.

This custom Model A Ford woodie uses the cowl and doors from a Tudor.

This restored Pontiac woodie shows the beauty of wood combined with perfect paint, wide whites, and lots of chrome.

A bear claw latch and a power window mechanism make up the inside of this custom woodie door. Doors need to be built sturdy to withstand thousands of slammings and the abuse rough roads can cause.

Here is a 1919 Pan automobile with its skin removed. The wood body framing provided excellent patterns but was in such bad shape that the dash rail was the only piece salvaged for the new body frame.

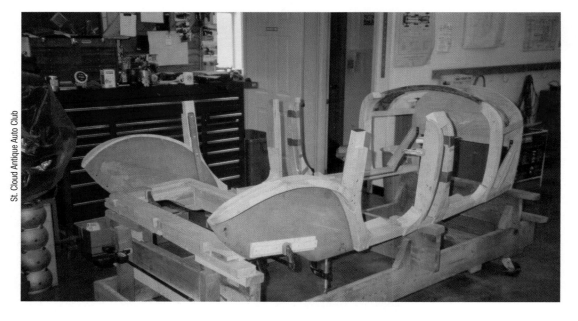

The Pan during the body frame rebuild. Notice the dark-colored dash rail, the only piece of the original frame that was salvageable.

Ready for its new clothes, this is one of only a dozen Pan autos in existence.

Jim Dugué

A stock vintage door latch is quite different from a modern one.

A simple flat bracket ties the door post to the roof rail. This type of bracket could easily be fabricated from sheet steel.

Jim Dugué

This more complex bracket ties the rear quarter post to the top rail and rear header. These are usually cast pieces in vintage cars but could easily be constructed from sheet steel welded together.

Jim Dugué

Rails, headers, bows, slats, and brackets combine to make this 1940 Plymouth top structure ready for its exterior upholstery. Top framing will consume a lot of time, as two wood screws should be used at each top slat/top bow intersection, but the results are breathtaking.

Jim Dugué

A windshield header, built up from several pieces of wood, is one of the more complex pieces in a woodie body. The back edge of the header has a rabbet for the top slats to fit into, forming a flush fit for the top upholstery to cover.

This 1940 Plymouth has steel wheelwells combined with a wooden floor. Notice the unique spare-tire mounting location.

The finger joint is used to make large pieces from small pieces or...

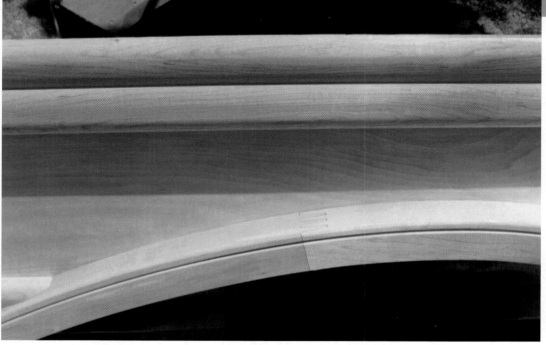

...long pieces from short. The finger joint provides a method for joining wood at angles and provides an end-grain-to-end-grain joint that is strong and good looking.

Glue

Call it glue or adhesive, it sticks just the same. Generally the term *glue* refers to a material that is derived from natural products such as starches or proteins, while an *adhesive* is a material that is based on polymers that are chemically produced. I, like most people, use the terms glue and adhesive interchangeably. I refer to all of the products in this chapter as *glue*.

GLUE IS THE TIE THAT BINDS

Careful joinery and metal hardware will go a long way toward keeping a project in one piece, but to make the joints stay tight you need to glue them. Glue bonds the fibers of the wood and fills the tiny voids between the surfaces of the joint, providing structural integrity and distributing stresses through the joint to the surrounding wood. Glue's strength is in this mechanical/chemical bond. Excessive amounts of glue in a loose-fitting joint will produce a joint that can be brittle and subject to failure.

Glue that has the ability to make a good structural bond in loose fitting joints is referred to as gap filling. Epoxy, resorcinol, and urea resin glues have varying degrees of gap-filling ability, but the only one that I trust to be structurally gap filling is epoxy. High-quality epoxy tends to remain flexible, while some gap-filling glues tend to become brittle and may fracture.

OPEN TIME, CLAMP TIME, AND CURE TIME

Open time, clamp time, and cure time are terms used to describe the working characteristics of glue. Open time refers to the amount of time a person has to work with the glue before clamp pressure must be applied. Moving or repositioning the joint after the open time has elapsed can lead to disruption of the chemical bond and ultimately to failure of the glue joint. Clamp time is the amount of time the project must be under clamp pressure to assure complete bonding. Cure time refers to the length of time it takes for the glue to reach its maximum strength. Glue joints should be allowed to fully cure before heavy machine work is done, such as power planing or power shaping, to assure that the bond is not disturbed.

Open time is critical when determining the type of glue to use on your project. As an example, long open time is necessary when doing projects like bent lamination in which the glue will be exposed to the air, unclamped, for an extended period of time.

CHOOSING THE RIGHT GLUE

There are more than a dozen types of glue and hundreds of different brands on the market today. Many of these products will not work well for automotive woodwork or are not available in the retail marketplace. I will narrow the choices to those that are readily available through retail outlets or mail order and that will work in the high-stress and moisture-prone environment cars encounter. Choosing the correct adhesive helps glue-ups proceed smoothly and will ensure full structural strength and longevity of the glue joint. There is no single glue that is suitable for all situations, and it is a good practice to have an assortment of different glues on hand. Using the following glue descriptions and the accompanying chart should make it easy to determine which glue will work for the project at hand.

HIDE GLUE—SOME LIKE IT HOT, SOME LIKE IT COLD

Hide glue has a long history in woodworking, dating back to ancient Egypt and the pharaohs. Hide glue also has a long history with the automobile. A lot of wood was used in early automobile construction, and hide glue was used extensively as the glue holding that wood together. Since World War II, the use of hide glue has declined, as new synthetic polymers created glue that is more water-resistant and easier to use. For some time, however, automobile manufacturers continued to use hide glue for interior veneer work.

I have included hide glue in this book because it is the best glue to use when repairing parts that were originally bonded with hide glue. PVA glue will not stick to hide glue, and removing all the old hide glue from the repair area can be nearly impossible.

Traditional hide glue is purchased in dry, granular form, then mixed with water, and heated to about 150 degrees Fahrenheit, at which point it forms a gel and is ready for use. Made from the protein of animal hides, it has low water resistance but "grabs" quickly. It has a relatively short clamp time and is easy to repair. (See chapter 9 for more on using hide glue.)

Hot hide glue has other benefits, such as the ability to quickly bond veneer to the

Cyanoacrylate glue, commonly referred to as "super glue," is available from many manufacturers.

background wood (substrate), in a process known as hammer veneering, and it will hold reinforcing blocks in place without the need for clamping. Hot hide glue sets as it cools. By varying the viscosity of the hot hide glue, you can customize it to fit precise gluing needs. The thinner the glue, the slower it sets, giving reasonably long open times for repair work. Thick hide glue gels quickly and is great for work where a clamp would be impossible to use. Traditional hide glue has a short shelf life once it is mixed. Because it is a protein, mold will quickly start to grow on the glue and destroy its strength. A few days is about the maximum length of time hide glue will be usable after being mixed with water. In the granular state hide glue will last indefinitely if kept dry.

Liquid hide glue is ready to use right out of the bottle. It is premixed and has preservatives to keep it from deteriorating. Though not as versatile as hot hide glue, liquid hide glue does save a lot of hassle and is the easiest way to reglue projects that were originally bonded with hide glue.

Hide glue has fairly low gap-filling ability and tends to be a bit brittle when applied in a thick layer. Resistant to moderate heat and solvents, hide glue also has good shock resistance and will hold up to moderate moisture conditions. This is the traditional choice for interior woodwork on an automobile.

CYANOACRYLATE GLUE

Cyanoacrylate glue is great for small repair jobs. Known generically as super glue, it has the deserved reputation of being able to glue anything together, including fingers. It sets extremely fast, and quick repairs can be made without the need for clamping. A separate accelerator can be used to make the glue harden even faster, but I would not recommend its use as the strength of the glue may be altered and the accelerator makes the glue turn white, leaving an obvious glue line.

Available in several different viscosities, the thinnest cyanoacrylate glue has great wicking capabilities, making it ideal for repairing cracks in wood that are too tight to get regular glue into, such as stress cracks or end checking. I often use it to repair screw holes that have been softened by decay or overuse and can no longer hold a screw. Just a small amount of glue will wick into the surrounding wood and make it solid again. Heavier viscosity cyanoacrylate works well to fill small holes and cracks or hold parts together that do not have a perfect fit.

Not resilient enough to do large projects, it is handy for quickly gluing or repairing small areas. Cyanoacrylate glue has good moisture and heat resistance but becomes quite brittle when cured.

HOT MELT GLUE

Hot melt glue is not strong enough for permanent structural bonds. Inexpensive hobby-type hot melt glue is great for holding pieces together temporarily. I use hot melt for holding complex assemblies together while I test-fit them. Use a few dabs of glue and hand hold the joint together until the glue has cooled; no need for clamps. After test-fitting, gently pry the pieces apart and scrape any remaining glue off the wood.

Hot melt glue is also handy for making jigs and building mock-ups of parts out of plywood or cardboard. Poor solvent and shock resistance combined with no heat

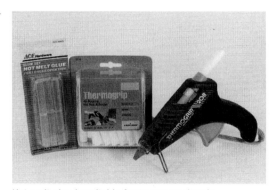

Hot melt glue is suitable for temporary bonds.

resistance relegates hot melt glue to general utility status.

PVA GLUE

Polyvinyl acetate glue or PVA is the most common glue found in the average woodshop today. Widely available, inexpensive, with a long shelf life, PVA comes in two forms: low grade and high grade. White normally denotes low grade, while yellow is usually the higher-grade product. The actual color has nothing to do with the strength of the glue. Yellow PVA is colored yellow as an easy way for manufacturers to distinguish it from its lower-strength sibling. Yellow glue is often referred to as aliphatic resin glue, although this is a meaningless marketing term used to help identify the higher-grade PVA glue.

Yellow glue has reasonable moisture resistance and low glue creep, which is the tendency glue can have to expand and extend beyond the joint creating a small ridge. Yellow glue is ideal for laminating interior wood pieces. Type II PVA, such as

PVA glue is available in regular, waterproof, and extended open-time formulas.

Titebond II, has very good shock resistance, is very water-resistant, and will work well for the exterior glue joints on an automobile. The only real drawback to using PVA is that under intense sunlight exposure, it tends to gradually degrade.

White PVA glue is generally considered low-grade hobby glue with adequate holding strength but is not well suited for the high-vibration and high-stress environment of automobiles.

PVA glue is thermoplastic, which means that heat above 150 degrees Fahrenheit will soften the glue. This makes it a bit hard to sand with power sanders, as the glue tends to plug the sanding belts and discs. Careful cleanup with water immediately after glue-up and scraping away any excess glue before sanding will help avoid problems.

Open time can vary according to the temperature and humidity in the shop. During hot summer weather or in a well-heated shop in the winter, you should be ready to assemble the joint quickly once the glue is applied, as the open time can drop to around 5 minutes.

Franklin International's Titebond glue, both PVA and PVA II, is available in extended open time formulas. This formula, makes long glue-ups, such as stack laminations, easier to accomplish without the worry of losing the integrity of the glue joint.

PVA glue is not a good gap-filling glue but in a good fitting glue joint, it is probably the best all-around, easiest-to-use product available. I use PVA almost exclusively, consigning the other glues to specialty usage.

POLYURETHANE GLUE

Polyurethane is an interesting glue. As the glue cures, any squeeze-out expands into plastic foam. This foaming characteristic makes the glue unacceptable as a gap-filling glue, as the strength of the foam is negligible. Polyurethane is best suited for tight joinery, and a little glue goes a long way. Usually about half the amount of glue that you would use if using a PVA glue will be the right amount to use, and the pieces must be well clamped to keep the expansion of the polyurethane from pushing things apart. A little experimentation with some scrap will quickly show how much to use.

Polyurethane has a fairly long open time, making it suitable for a prolonged glue-up of tight joinery, such as edge laminating or stack laminating boards. Although not completely waterproof, it does have very good water resistance and is very resistant to high heat, solvents, and shock loading.

To hasten the set-up time of the glue, a light mist of water on the surfaces prior to glue-up will significantly speed up the process, as water is the catalyst for polyurethane. Working in a heated shop in the winter can dry wood to the point of virtually no moisture on the wood surface. In a situation such as this, it is advisable to dampen the wood just to get the glue to catalyze.

Very good heat resistance makes polyurethane a good glue to use in areas subjected to high temperatures.

UREA RESIN GLUE

Urea resin glue is available in one-part and two-part formulas. The one-part formula mixes a powdered resin with water, while the two-part formula mixes a liquid resin with a powdered catalyst. For optimum performance there is a recommended mixture ratio of catalyst to resin, but for special situations when a longer or shorter open time is desired, the glue can be mixed slightly off ratio without significantly lowering its performance. One-part urea resin is generally easier to use, but the two-part formulas tend to be better performers.

Also referred to as urea-formaldehyde glue, urea resin glue is a good choice for high-stress environments. Moderate gap-filling capabilities make it good for gluing less than perfect joints. Easy to sand after curing, urea is very resistant to heat and solvents and has fairly good shock resistance, although some lower-priced urea resin may tend to become brittle with age. Buy the best you can find.

High water resistance makes urea resin a good glue for exterior joinery but a dark glue line and possible staining of the wood, especially very light-colored wood such as maple, make accurate joinery and immediate glue cleanup necessary. Uncured urea resin cleans up easily with warm water and a cloth or sponge. Unibond 800 glue is available with different colored catalysts to help disguise joint lines.

RESORCINOL

Resorcinol glue is the dark purplish

Urea resin glue is waterproof, gap-filling, and easy to work with. A relatively long open time makes complex glue-ups, such as laminate bending, easier.

glue often used in marine plywood and structural laminated beams. Waterproof and very strong, with high shock resistance and good solvent and heat resistance, it is glue that is ideally suited for exterior structural use. Its biggest drawback is its dark color. Glue lines show up as almost black lines.

This would be good glue to use for any wood in a car that will see lots of moisture, heat, and vibration, such as floorboards or structural body bracing. It will also work well for any substructure pieces, such as support blocks for window risers and door latches, where the assembly is hidden beneath cover panels.

EPOXY

Epoxy is probably the ultimate glue for exterior woodwork on an automobile. It is waterproof, clear, and can even be used as a top coat. There are literally hundreds of epoxies available in the marketplace. Five-minute epoxies are great for small repairs or for gluing dissimilar materials such as aluminum and wood. Long-cure epoxies are the best for automotive use, as they tend to be the strongest. T-88 is my favorite epoxy. It is considered a structural adhesive and it will cure in low temperatures, making it ideal for use in shops that tend to be a bit cool in the middle of the winter, which is usually when most of us have time to work on our projects. T-88 is also very good for bonding dissimilar surfaces such as aluminum or steel to wood. This ability can be

Epoxy is waterproof and gap filling, and it dries clear, making glue lines that are virtually invisible.

Remove the foam from an inexpensive foam brush and you have a dandy glue spreader. The plastic can be trimmed to produce profiled spreaders, and most dried glues can be removed by simply flexing the plastic.

a real asset for bedding metal hardware, increasing the strength of the hardware, and waterproofing the connection to help keep water damage at bay.

Strong, flexible, and waterproof, epoxy has good structural gap-filling capabilities. A variety of additives are available for epoxy to help make it a great gap-filling glue. Phenolic microballoons, silica thickener, and wood flour are some of the products available to modify epoxy for specialized applications. Microballoons mixed with epoxy will produce a firm, lightweight paste that is excellent for fairing surfaces that are to be painted or veneered over. Wood flour will make the epoxy a color-matching (in light-colored wood), nonsagging paste that will work great for filling cracks or gaps in exposed joinery work. Silica thickener mixed with epoxy will create a soft paste that is suitable for use as a gap-filling glue.

All epoxy glue is two part and must be mixed thoroughly before use. Varying the catalyst-to-resin ratio can slow or speed the working, known as reaction time, making epoxy very versatile. System Three epoxy has several different catalysts specifically developed for different reaction and cure rates. Using these catalysts, rather than modifying ratios, will result in more

consistent results. Cool temperatures can affect the setup and curing of epoxy, so make sure you read the instructions and be aware of what the minimum working temperature of the epoxy is. In cold conditions, it can take a very long time for the epoxy to set up. Lacquer thinner can be used to thin epoxy. Epoxy is messy to work with, so make sure you have throwaway latex gloves and lacquer thinner on hand. Wax paper will work great to keep epoxy off the face of clamps and clamp pads. Cleaning up glue squeeze-out immediately after clamp-up will save a lot of difficult scraping later on.

SOME TIPS, TRICKS, AND SPECIAL TOOLS

I use a handy little plastic glue spreader that is cheap and easily modified for special application needs. The spreader is a cheap foam brush with the foam removed. Under the foam is a stiff plastic backer that holds the foam to the wood handle. The plastic is easily trimmed for special applications and most adhesives can be removed from the plastic by simply bending the plastic after the adhesive has dried. I have three spreaders of different widths—3/4 inch for spreading glue on the edges of boards, 1-1/4 inch for general glue-up work, and 2 inch for big glue-ups, such as laminating plywood together or other projects where I need to spread a lot of glue in a hurry.

When I have a lot of PVA or epoxy to spread for laminating or veneering, I use a 4-inch foam roller. The rollers are cheap so they can be tossed after the glue-up, and it's easy to get a good, even coat of glue on the wood.

The best time to remove the glue from panels and exposed joints is after it has set but before it cures. Cured glue tends to take little chunks of wood with it when it is scraped off. If the glue is too wet, it makes a smeary mess to try to clean up. A good paint scraper works well for removing excess glue. Keep the scraper sharp and round the corners off so there is less chance for the corners to dig into the work.

Glue squeeze-out in areas that are hard to access should be cleaned up immediately after clamping. PVA, hide, resorcinol, and urea resin glue can be cleaned up with water. Epoxy cleans up easily with lacquer thinner, alcohol, or acetone. Polyurethane and cyanoacrylate will clean up with acetone. Use a cotton cloth and enough solvent to get all of the glue residue off the wood. Glue smears and stains will show up when staining or finishing, so do a good cleanup job.

TOO MUCH OR NOT ENOUGH

The ideal amount of glue used in a lamination is enough to wet the surfaces and provide a good bond

PVA glue, hide glue, urethane glue, and cyanoacrylate glue like a good tight fit of the pieces, as they are not good at filling gaps. PVA and hide glue should be applied to the amount that a fine line or small beads of squeeze-out appear when clamp pressure is applied. There is no benefit to having so much glue in the joint that it runs out all over the work surface. Excess glue is messy and can cause problems at finish time, so it needs to be cleaned up as soon as the work is in the clamps.

Cyanoacrylate is best applied sparingly. Because of its low viscosity, it has a tendency to run everywhere. I like to have the parts that I am bonding with cyanoacrylate in contact with each other, let the glue seep into the glue line until the glue line is filled, then apply clamp pressure. Clean up the excess glue quickly.

Urethane should be applied at about one-third the rate of yellow glue, as it expands as it catalyzes. Wait until the glue has cured before cleaning off the excess. The excess glue will become a rigid foam that is easy to trim off with a sharp chisel.

None of these glues are gap filling, so accurate joinery is a must for strong bonds between the glue and the wood.

Urea resin and resorcinol work well with a tight fit, but can also be used if the fit is less than perfect. Both have some gap-filling capabilities, although large gaps will not have much structural integrity. Again, a thin squeeze-out line indicates a sufficient amount of glue is being used. Urea resin is my choice for any exterior joinery because of its water resistance and slight gap-filling qualities.

Epoxy is the one glue that can benefit from a less-than-perfect joint. Some epoxy manufacturers recommend that a close-fitting joint not be clamped too tightly or the joint might be starved for glue and end up having a weak bond. I only use epoxy to glue ill-fitting joints or to make repairs.

GLUING PROBLEM WOOD

Many tropical hardwoods such as rosewood and ebony have a lot of natural oil in the fibers. Oil and glue won't stick together. Just before applying the glue to the wood, wipe the surface with acetone, which will remove enough of the oil near the surface of the wood to allow the glue to bond with the wood fibers. Immediately apply glue to the cleaned surfaces and clamp up the pieces. Urea resin, resorcinol, and epoxy glue will work better with oily wood than PVA.

Edge Gluing

Apply a nice even bead of glue to the edge of the board.

Use a glue spreader to distribute the glue evenly over the entire surface.

Apply clamp pressure. A small amount of glue squeeze-out indicates a good glue joint. Excessive glue can produce a weak joint.

SHELF LIFE

Most glues have a reasonably long shelf life. PVA glue should be good for a couple of years. As it ages, it becomes thick and stringy; time for the trash. Powdered glues will outlast liquid glues for the simple reason that they don't have solvents that will evaporate over time.

Keep glue in dark, cool storage. Glue that is exposed to heat and sunlight will deteriorate rapidly. Glue that has been frozen will still work if it is brought to room temperature before using. PVA glue that has been frozen may become lumpy or stringy. If I accidentally allow my PVA glue to freeze, I usually pitch it and use fresh glue. Trying to save a few bucks isn't worth endangering a whole project.

Repairing and Restoring Old Wood and Veneer

Replacing damaged wood is not always an option when restoring an old car. Sometimes it is not even desired. There are ways of repairing old wood that has suffered damage without tearing the car apart to replace the piece. If the car has significant historical or sentimental value, it's important to keep as much of the original wood intact as possible.

CYANOACRYLATE GLUE GIVES THE CREEPS

Cyanoacrylate glue, commonly referred to as super slue, has extremely low viscosity, allowing it to penetrate deeply into cracked or rotted wood. Apply enough glue to completely saturate the damaged wood. The glue can be cured quickly with the use of a spray catalyst (accelerator) which can really help if a lot of glue is needed to fill the cracks or damaged wood. Cyanoacrylate glue makes a good primer for epoxy. Once the wood has been stabilized and solidified, epoxy can be added to rebuild the wood.

Wood that has stress cracks can be repaired with cyanoacrylate glue. I often use this glue to repair run-out cracks in wood. The glue has such low viscosity that it will pull itself all the way to the end of a crack, providing a complete repair of the crack. This is a real benefit when a crack appears while machining a new piece of wood. Instead of trying to pry the crack open to get ordinary glue in, you can use cyanoacrylate glue, and let it wick into the crack, eliminating the chance of further damage.

PATCHING WOOD WITH NEW WOOD AND EPOXY

If most of the wood on a piece is good, often a patch can be grafted to the existing piece, saving time and money.

A scarf joint or a lap joint, when combined with epoxy, can produce a joint strong enough to mend or replace bad wood. This is a hard joint to make cosmetically perfect but it can make a great utility repair, if function is more important than fashion. Epoxy is a good gap-filling glue. In fact, epoxy manufacturers recommend that the parts not fit too tightly, or too much epoxy will be squeezed out of the joint, starving the joint for glue and producing a weak bond. If you have a patch repair that is difficult to clamp properly, use epoxy to produce a strong repair. I have held repair pieces in place with masking tape and have gotten a very satisfactory glue bond using epoxy this way.

Don't buy the cheapest brand of epoxy. My favorite is T-88, a structural epoxy that is not as fussy about temperature as some epoxies and is extremely strong. Try to avoid using 5-minute epoxies, as they just don't seem to have the strength of a long-cure epoxy. Five-minute epoxies are best

Polyester body filler tinted with artist oils produces a filler that will blend with the surrounding wood and won't shrink or crack.

for quick repairs that aren't intended to be permanent or aren't subjected to the high stress of automotive use.

POLYESTER BODY FILLER IS GOOD FOR WOOD BODIES TOO

I have used polyester filler, generically known as Bondo, for years as wood filler. The filler bonds to wood incredibly well, doesn't shrink or crack, is waterproof, can be easily shaped, and will hold a screw. Polyester filler can even be tinted with artist oils or universal tint colorants to match the surrounding wood. If the patch is small, say filling a nonoriginal hole or repairing a gouge, body filler will work well enough to be a cosmetic repair if tinted to match the surrounding wood.

Use a white filler and white cream hardener. Tinting the hardener is much easier when you don't have to start with a gray filler, the most common type sold.

Blue or red hardeners just won't make a very good match for maple or mahogany.

To fine-tune a Bondo repair, use a little wood stain to help feather the color of the filler into the surrounding wood. I even add a few stripes of woodgrain using artist oils and a fine artist's brush. With a little practice, you can make a repair disappear.

EPOXY FILLS THE VOIDS AND CAN REPAIR ROT TO BOOT

If structural integrity is the goal of repairing wood, there are two products that can bring that integrity back to damaged wood. Keep in mind the wood will never be "as good as new" but it can be made serviceable again and in places where cosmetics don't count, that is all that's necessary.

System Three has a product called Sculpwood that is designed for replacing missing wood. Sculpwood is epoxy-based, moldable, and after being cured it can be sanded or shaped and holds a screw well. If you are looking for a quick fix that does not need to be cosmetic, this is the ticket.

RotFix is another System Three product that can save a lot of hassle and time. RotFix is a low-viscosity epoxy that is designed to consolidate rotted, deteriorated, or damaged wood. The low viscosity allows it to penetrate deep into damaged wood, providing good strength. This is a great product for repairing noncosmetic problems where replacing the wood is difficult, such as a metal-wrapped door post like those Chevy was famous for.

A good trick to use when working with RotFix is to drill small holes in the affected wood. These holes will help the RotFix penetrate the wood more quickly and more completely. Warming the RotFix before applying it to the damaged wood will help the penetration also, but keep in mind that the warmth will also cause the epoxy to catalyze faster.

Using RotFix to stabilize and strengthen damaged wood, combined with Sculpwood to replace missing wood, makes noncosmetic repairs relatively easy

System Three provides a number of products specifically designed for repairing damaged wood. Its T-88 is one of the best epoxies available.

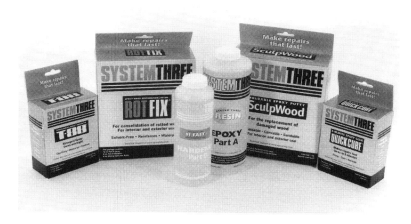

and permanent, provided the source of the wood's damage is corrected.

There are other epoxy products on the market that are supposed to be very effective at stabilizing rotted or damaged wood. System Three is the product I am familiar with, so it is the product that I recommend.

A variety of additives, such as phenolic microballoons, wood flour, and silica thickener may be added to regular epoxy to produce a thick, nonsagging paste that can be used for repairing medium-sized gaps and cracks.

SPLICING BROKEN OR ROTTEN WOOD

Certain body parts, such as wheel arches and the framing under the top fabric, are more prone to rotting than the rest of a car. A splice can often save a piece of wood that is mostly sound but has perhaps a bit of rot or some accident damage.

If the piece can be removed from the car, make a pattern of the piece before you remove the damaged section. A pattern will assure that the repaired piece is the same dimension and shape as the original and can be used during glue-up of the repair to keep everything in line.

Cut out all of the damaged wood, leaving at least an 8-to-1 bevel on the ends of the sound wood. A tapered joint such as this is called a scarf joint and is often used to join wood in boat building. If the repair is cosmetic as well as structural, choose a piece of repair wood similar in color and grain to match the repair. Cut the exact bevel on each end of the splice and glue the splice into place. An easy way to ensure the bevels are accurate and will match the bevels on the patch piece is to use a bevel block to guide the chisel for the final bevel cuts. Make an 8-to-1 block by laying out the bevel on a piece of hardwood and then cut it with the band saw, table saw, or a handsaw. Dress the surface smooth and flat with a block plane and use a little beeswax or candle wax to give it a nice slick face. This sloped face will be a guide to lay your

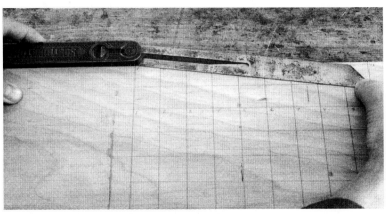

chisel blade on to make the precise bevel cuts for your splice. Most of the waste wood can be removed up to the layout line by eye using the bevel block for just the last few shavings.

If you are careful in fitting the bevel and use a splice that is oversized in width and height, you can trim the excess material and have a repair that is cosmetically acceptable as well as mechanically sound.

Scarf joints are good for repairing parts that can't be easily removed from the car. The damaged portion of the part can be removed and the bevels cut using a sharp chisel, a guide block, and good layout lines. The splice will have to fit the adjoining surfaces accurately but should still be oversized to give some allowance for trimming to exact size.

Half-lap joints can also be used to repair damage, although a half-lap joint does not have the strength of a well-made scarf joint.

Another method that I have found effective is to use a belt sander to make a curved recess in the wood and then laminate thin layers of wood into the depression allowing the ends of the layers to extend beyond the surface of the repair. When the glue has cured, sand the ends flush with the surrounding surface. This method does not need precise bevels so is a little easier to perform for novice woodworkers.

Urea resin is probably the best glue for this application, as it has gap-filling capabilities. Waterproof carpenter's glue such as Titebond II would work, as long as the parts fit tight.

Use a sliding T-bevel to lay out an 8-to-1 bevel. The length of the bevel essentially forms a scarf joint.

INSTALLING SISTER FRAMES OR DOUBLERS

Here's another old boat building trick. Boats have lots of frame members holding the hull together. Sister frames, also known as doublers, are fastened alongside damaged frames, restoring the strength of the original frame. In a woodie or wooden-framed body, there are many places where a sister frame could repair the strength of the body when cosmetics aren't a concern.

A sister frame can be fastened with screws or can be glued to the damaged frame member. Make sure that the sister frame is sufficiently sized to give the original strength back to the frame. Epoxy is probably the best adhesive to use in this repair as it is often hard to get a tight fit between the parts.

This is definitely a utility repair and can only be considered when the repair is out of sight, hidden under panels or upholstery. Not pretty to look at but very functional, sistering can save a lot of time and money and help keep an old original body from deteriorating due to loss of structural strength.

REPAIRING VENEER

Carpathian elm burl, walnut burl, and bird's-eye maple are beautiful veneers that, when combined with fine leather and wool carpeting, become the very essence of classic car interiors. These rare veneers are incredibly elegant when covered with a "mile-deep" gloss finish. Rare, beautiful, and unfortunately, rather fragile.

A car's interior environment is often detrimental to solid wood and catastrophic to veneer. As long as a good finish is kept on veneered pieces, the veneer will usually remain solidly fastened to the substrate. Many old cars, unfortunately, have had little upkeep, and once the finish is gone, water and sun conspire to destroy the fragile bond between the veneer and its substrate.

Veneer is not as difficult to repair as some would have you believe. Patience is probably the most important resource a person needs to muster for an effective repair.

STABILIZING THE PATIENT

The first thing that you want to do when dealing with old veneered pieces is to stabilize the damage and protect the veneer from further damage. Usually portions of the veneer have lost their bond with the substrate and are literally hanging on by a thread. Try to save as much of this loose veneer as possible. It is easier to repair loose veneer than to match and splice new veneer in its place. Matching old veneer with new veneer can be very hard and the less you have to replace the better. In many instances all of the veneer in an interior came from the same piece of wood with perfect color and grain match. Unless the veneer is absolutely destroyed, it is worth preserving.

Until I can get the piece out of the car and onto my workbench, I use blue masking tape or clear shelf paper to hold the loose veneer in place. The blue tape and shelf paper do not hold as tenaciously as regular masking tape and will separate from the veneer without tearing it apart. Handle the veneer carefully; it is very delicate and you want to save as much of it as you can.

The next step is to find out what kind of glue was used to hold the veneer. (Old-fashioned hide glue seems to be the glue of choice for most British cars.) A simple water test will immediately show if the glue is hide glue. Take a small artist's brush or cotton swab and wipe down a small area under the veneer with water. After a few minutes, feel the wet area to see if it is sticky or at least slimy. The water will reconstitute the hide glue, if any is still on the wood, no matter how old the glue is. If there is no evidence of glue on the wood and the water test doesn't reveal anything, try gently lifting some of the veneer away from the substrate. If there is a lot of loose veneer, lift off as much as you can beginning at a corner. Use a thin putty knife and gently lift the veneer off. Try the water test again. If there is still no stick or slime, the glue is probably a PVA or urea resin glue.

If you determine hide glue was not used, you will have to use a modern glue to repair the veneer. I find that PVA will stick sufficiently to any substrate, except substrate tainted with hide glue. That's why I usually use PVA to fix loose veneer. Simply smear the glue under the loose veneer using a thin blade putty knife or a recipe card. Then place a sheet of wax paper over the repair area and cover it with a board as big as the repair. Clamp the board tight to the veneered surface.

If the veneer is only loose in small areas and I'm unable to lift it from the substrate, I use cyanoacrylate glue. Cyanoacrylate's ability to wick under the veneer makes it a good choice. The glue will wick all the way to solidly adhered veneer, making the repair complete. Use a rounded dowel to burnish the veneer into the glue until it sets up. Cyanoacrylate sets quickly, so this won't be a real chore. You can tell if the veneer is stuck back down by lightly tapping on it. If the veneer sounds hollow, it is still loose and needs either more glue or more burnishing and drying time. If you have trouble getting the glue to wick under the veneer, cut a few slits along the grain using a sharp utility knife and apply the glue to those slits. The glue should disappear rather quickly. Keep adding more glue until it stands on top of the veneer. This will signal complete saturation of the loose area. Wipe off the excess and start burnishing. Be careful not to use too much pressure while burnishing. The veneer only has to be pushed into the glue and too much pressure may produce a dent.

HIDE GLUE REPAIRS

Veneer that was attached with hide glue can be rebonded using a clothes iron and a wet cotton cloth. Unless it has been devoured by fungi or other protein-eating critters, hide glue, an animal protein, can be reconstituted with water. If there is any hide glue left under the veneer, steam

Repairing Veneer with Hide Glue

This glue pot, brush and clamp needed to repair veneer with hide glue.

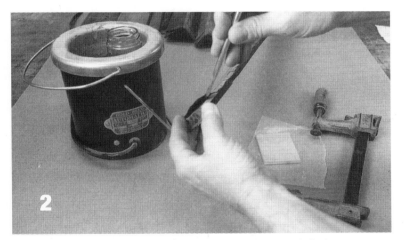

Use a small brush to apply the hide glue to the substrate beneath the loose veneer.

Use waxed paper under a clamp pad to keep the glue from sticking to the pad. The pad protects the wood from clamp damage and spreads the clamp pressure out, ensuring a better glue bond.

produced by the application of the hot iron to the wet cotton cloth will soften the old hide glue and cause it to stick again.

The process of ironing the veneer back down is delicate, and I advise you to experiment on some scrap first. Try to find an old piece of furniture that has loose veneer and practice on that before you try repairing your precious dashboard or window garnish molding. I have found that old dressers tend to have a lot of loose veneer and can be picked up in that condition for nearly nothing. If you iron all the veneer back down, not only do you gain a lot of experience but you also end up with a neat old dresser that you can refinish after the car is done. You could even use the dresser as a test bed for stripping, staining, and finishing.

If the hide glue has vanished from under the veneer, you will need to replace it with fresh hide glue. You can't use PVA or some other glue because these glues will not adhere to the remnants of the hide glue that will be present. It may seem that there is no glue left, but believe me, there is still enough in the grain of the wood to cause adhesion problems with another type of glue. I speak from experience!

If you have a lot of veneer to repair, buy some dried hide glue. I use Behlen's ground hide glue. There is very little odor from this brand and it dries exceptionally clear, making a nearly invisible glue line.

To use ground hide glue you have to emulsify the granules and heat the glue to a liquid. Use a small jar and add about one-third cup of granules. Add enough water to cover the granules and stir. Let the resulting mush sit for a half-hour or so, until the granules turn to jelly. Using a water-filled pan, place the jar in the water and heat to around 150 degrees. It will take about 20 minutes for the glue to liquefy. Remove the glue from the heat and allow it to cool. It will return to a gelatinous state. Reheat the glue, and it is ready to use. The glue should be about the consistency of thick cream. If the glue is too thick, simply add a small amount of water, but be sparing with the water as the glue will dilute quickly. If the glue is too thin, heat it for a while in an uncovered jar until enough water has evaporated to thicken the glue. The glue should be kept at 150 degrees all the while you are using it. Hide glue bonds as it cools, producing the initial bond after passing through the gel state. It reaches its final bond as it dehydrates or "dries."

An automatic glue pot that operates on the double boiler principle can be bought and is a good investment if you plan on using a lot of hide glue. I have been told that baby bottle warmers will work also, though I have never tried one. If you are only repairing the veneer for one restoration, save your money and use a pan on the stove. Or you could borrow a hot plate to use in the shop. The kitchen probably isn't the best place to work on old wooden car parts.

Once the glue is ready, spread it under the old veneer and use weights or clamps to hold the veneer in place until the glue sets up. I have used masking tape on pieces that are too oddly shaped to be clamped. If you use too much glue, the squeeze-out will glue the masking tape to the wood. But don't worry; it can be scraped off without damaging the veneer. Liquid hide glue is regular hide glue that has chemicals added to keep it from gelling when it's cool. Liquid hide glue is the same stuff as the hot hide glue and has the same holding power, but I prefer the hot hide glue. Hot hide glue softens the veneer and helps it flatten back down to the substrate. There is something satisfying about the whole process of working with hot hide glue that I enjoy too.

Hide glue has quite a history and can be traced back to the earliest woodworking. Furniture in ancient Egypt was held together with hide glue. Working with hide glue is experiencing technology that has been around for a long, long time.

PATCHING VENEER

No matter how careful you are with old veneer, there are times when you run into a project where the material is too damaged or missing altogether. Patching veneer is not impossible; it just takes time and patience.

The easiest veneers to patch are the burls. Matching the wild grain patterns, or at least hiding the patch, is a lot easier than trying to match straight-grained veneer. The important thing to look for is the density of the figure itself. The color of the veneer can always be altered, as long as the all of the swirls and "eyes" look appropriate.

I have often taken a small sample of the veneer and sent it to my veneer supplier for them to match. They have access to lots of different flitches of veneer and can compare the sample to their stock, hopefully finding a good match.

Cut the patch first. Irregular-shaped patches are easier to hide than rectilinear patches. Try to find natural curving grain to use as cut lines for making the patch. Once the patch piece is cut, glue it to the damaged area with rubber cement. The rubber cement will hold the piece steady as a line is scribed exactly around the edge of the patch. Scribe very lightly the first time around the patch and then increase the pressure with each succeeding pass until you have cut through the veneer. Using a thin-bladed putty knife, carefully lift the patch off. Remove the damaged veneer, using the scribed line as a stop cut. A very sharp chisel or an 1/8-inch straight bit in a minirouter will do a good job of removing the waste. Apply glue to the repair area and push the patch into the fresh glue. I often use a few bits of blue masking tape to keep the patch from shifting. Cover the patch with wax paper and a clamping caul and apply clamp pressure sufficient to flatten the patch.

After the glue has dried, remove the clamp and carefully sand the new veneer flush with the surrounding veneer. Keep in mind that the surrounding veneer is extremely thin, especially if it has been refinished at some time in the past, and sand slowly and very cautiously. Keep watch for any signs of sand-through. Be patient.

Carefully trim away any ragged veneer on the edges of the patch. An irregularly shaped patch will be less visible than a straight-edged one.

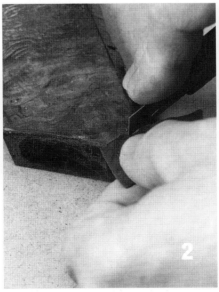

Use the wallpaper method of cutting through both layers of veneer at the same time to get a perfect fit.

The finished patch is virtually invisible. Careful veneer matching is the key to a good veneer patch.

Refinishing and Restoring Wood

Refinishing wood is like a birthday party with the gifts all wrapped and ready to open. Old varnish or paint is not as pretty as nice wrapping paper, but the gift that waits to be unwrapped is just as exciting as any birthday present. I always find it a thrill when the old finish starts coming off to reveal beautiful woodgrain beneath.

TYPES OF STRIPPERS

The quickest way to remove an old finish is with paint stripper. Paint stripper will remove paint, polyurethane, shellac, and lacquer with a minimum of effort and without damaging the wood beneath the old finish. It is a messy job but the results will be worth the effort.

I have found that the most effective stripper is the type with methylene chloride as the active ingredient. Methylene chloride will remove virtually any finish, is nonflam-

mable, and works from the bottom up, saturating the old finish and lifting it off the surface of the wood. Great care must be taken while using this type of stripper, as methylene chloride is a known carcinogen, and breathing the fumes is very dangerous. Standard paint respirators **will not** handle methylene chloride fumes, so the best place to use the stripper is outdoors or in a well-ventilated area. Keep a pail of water handy just in case you accidentally get stripper on your bare skin. Wear chemical-resistant gloves, a solvent-proof or acid-proof apron, and safety glasses. Methylene chloride works great but it is just plain nasty stuff, so be careful and treat it with respect.

Now that we have all the nasty stuff considered, we can move on to the real wonder of stripper, its ability to remove decades of crusty varnish or paint in a matter of minutes.

STRIPPING PROCEDURES

The best way to apply stripper is to spray it on. Stripper has a wax mixed in that will float to the top of the applied stripper and help keep evaporation to a minimum. Without this wax cover, the stripper would evaporate before it could do its work. Brushing the stripper is possible, but it is hard to get consistent coverage and rebrushing simply pushes the wax down into the stripper, making the stripper less effective.

The basic paint and varnish removal kit includes scrapers, wire brushes, shave hooks, and "pointy things" to help get the gunk off the wood.

Using a sprayer to apply the stripper provides an even coat and allows the wax in the stripper to do an effective job of keeping it from evaporating.

I use Dad's Easy Spray stripper. Although it can be applied with the plastic spray bottle supplied with the stripper, I prefer to use my Sure Shot brass-canister Model A sprayer, which is an all-metal, reusable, pressurized sprayer that does a great job of applying the rather thick stripper. The brass canister will not rust from exposure to the chemicals, which is a very important consideration. Fill the can about two-thirds full of stripper, pressurize to about 100 psi, and you are ready to go. You will need to refill the sprayer with compressed air several times for one fill of stripper. The advantage of this sprayer is that it will lay an even coat of stripper over the surface without leaving thin areas that dry out quickly.

Cover the wood with a good heavy coat of stripper. If you can lay the piece horizontally you can get a thicker coat of stripper but if the piece must remain vertical, try not to put such a heavy coat on so that the stripper runs. Remember the stripper has to stay in place to do its job.

Let the stripper sit on the wood until the paint or varnish can easily be scraped off with a putty knife. If the stripper starts to dry out before the finish is loosened from the wood, simply add more stripper. In some instances, I have had to reapply the stripper several times over a couple of hours to get the finish to part company with the wood. Paint is the worst offender, especially if it was applied over bare wood.

A good painter would always remove the old varnish before priming and painting the wood. A poor painter would paint right over the varnish. I am sure glad there were so many poor painters years ago!

When the finish is loose, remove the stripper with a flexible-bladed putty knife. I do a little fine-tuning on my putty knives that I use for removing stripper; I round the corners to help keep the knife from digging into the wood as I remove the stripper. Have a couple of different widths on hand: wide for large surfaces such as door panels, and narrow for window frames and small panels. I also have a scratch awl with a slightly narrowed tip, a short-bladed carver's knife, and a set of shave hooks for cleaning grooves and concave surfaces.

Number 1 medium steel wool is the next tool in a stripper's arsenal. Scotch-Brite scrub pads work too, but they fill up with residue more quickly than steel wool. A steel wool pad can be unrolled to expose a clean fresh surface. Dip the steel wool in lacquer thinner, mineral spirits, or alcohol, and proceed to scrub the residue off the wood's surface. If there are still areas where

Carefully scrape the stripper and old paint or varnish off the wood. Sometimes a second coat may be needed to get the pieces clean. Make sure to wear chemical-proof gloves and have a good supply of fresh air.

Wash the stripped wood with mineral spirits or alcohol to remove the stripper residue. The result will be a clean surface ready for refinishing.

the finish is not completely removed, simply reapply the stripper and go through the process again. It is easier and more effective to coat a piece entirely with stripper and attempt to remove all the finish at once. Sometimes not all of the finish comes off, but the first coating will make it easier for subsequent coats to do their job. Cleaning the residue off is easiest when it is still soft from the stripper. If you walk away from the project before it is clean, you will need to reapply stripper to the entire surface again to get it clean, so only tackle an area that you are sure you can get done in the time you have available to work on it.

Again I would like to impress the importance of having adequate airflow around the work area. Strippers and thinners are dangerous to breathe, and thinner can be explosive if concentrations are high and an ignition source is present. A good quality paint respirator will work with thinners but won't be effective with methylene chloride. Be careful.

REPAIRING BARE WOOD

After all the old finish has been removed, it's time to get the wood surface ready for its next finish. Scratches, dents, stains, and other damage can be removed or repaired when the wood is bare.

Dents can usually be removed or at least greatly reduced with steam. I use an old clothes iron for this task. Set the iron to the cotton or wool setting. Wet a clean cotton cloth with clean water and lay the cloth over the dent. Apply heat with the iron, which will drive the steam into the wood, swelling the grain and raising the dent. Don't let the cloth dry out or you may scorch the wood. When the steam stops, remove the cloth immediately and check your progress. It usually takes several applications of steam to remove a dent, so be patient. Some dents are just too deep or have been in the wood too long to be effectively removed, but at least they can be minimized by steaming.

Deep scratches are tough to remove. Steam won't work on most deep scratches, because the grain of the wood has been severed and the interlocking ends of the severed grain won't allow the wood to swell back to its original shape. Most scratches have to be sanded out. Make sure you feather the sanded area into the surrounding wood so that you don't end up with a dip. The process is similar to sanding away a paint chip or scratch. If the scratch is too deep or in a place where removal is impossible, it needs to be filled.

There are many wood fillers on the market, but I prefer to use products that are not often thought of as wood fillers. My favorite fillers are epoxy and polyester body filler (generically referred to as Bondo). Most epoxies dry clear or light amber and can do a great job of filling scratches if the wood is not going to be stained. Epoxy is not porous and will not accept a stain. I have mixed sawdust with epoxy to fill larger cracks or scratches and it works well although it's not invisible. Make sure you use sawdust from the same species of wood being repaired.

Body filler works great for scratches, cracks, and holes and can even be used for filling the woodgrain if a filled grain finish is desired. The great thing about body filler is its ability to be colored. I keep a selection of artist oils on hand to tint the filler to match the wood. A little experimentation will give you the basics for coloring filler. As an example, I have found that a little raw sienna mixed with the filler will produce a light tan color that blends well with red oak. Add a touch of blue and you can match white oak and green ash. Raw sienna, white, and just a tiny touch of Alizarin red will match old maple. With some practice you can become a regular Rembrandt with body filler.

Keep in mind that any filler will fill the woodgrain surrounding the scratch or hole and when finish is applied, this area will be shinier than the surrounding grain. I usually mask off the repair with masking tape, keeping the filler out of everything except the repair. This makes it easier to sand the filler flush also.

SANDING THE WOOD

After all of the repairs have been performed, it is time to get the surface smooth.

I usually start sanding with 80-grit sandpaper if there is a lot of gray, sun-bleached wood that needs to be removed. I use a random-orbit sander (disc sanders are too aggressive) and sand all of the wood at the same time. After the rough stuff has been removed, I use compressed air to blow off all of the accumulated sawdust and sanding grit. I switch to 100-grit, repeat the process, and finish up with 150-grit, which is fine enough for a great finish.

Be careful with the panels. The panels on a woodie are usually veneered and the veneer is extremely thin. Hand sand the panels. If the panels are in rough shape, they will need to be replaced. If the panels are in good shape, a light hand sanding will be all that's necessary. If you use a power sander on the panels, especially with coarse-grit paper, you will probably end up damaging them, and veneer is very hard to repair.

After using the orbital on all of the pieces, I do a final sanding by hand. Using a small sanding block, the hard rubber type that body shops use, I sand all of the surfaces, following the direction of the grain, with 150-grit paper. This process assures that I have eliminated any possible swirl scratches left by the random-orbit sander.

The last sanding process is to ease all of the hard edges. Finish will not stick to a knife-edge and after extensive sanding or repair work you may find many knife-edges on your project. I use 150-grit paper and hand sand the edges being careful not to leave sanding scratches on the surrounding surfaces.

This process may seem fussy but it is essential to a good finish. As with body-work, the finished product depends on good preparation work and attention to detail. Take your time and do the best job you possibly can. It is a lot of work to redo a finish, and you want to be happy with the results after expending so much effort.

Be sure to wear a dust mask, as sanding dust can be a respiratory irritant. Besides, a dust mask just makes the job a little more pleasant.

REMOVING COLOR AND STAINS

After years of exposure to sun and rain, wood often acquires various stains. Some of these stains are caused by fungi and are permanent; others are caused by contact with iron and can be removed or

Here is a typical iron oxide stain on a piece of white ash. I created the stain by leaving a piece of wet steel wool on the wood overnight. It is amazing how black an iron oxide stain can get.

I used a cotton cloth soaked in oxalic acid to remove the stain. I actually left the saturated cloth on the surface of the wood for several hours. When the stain has been completely removed, it is a good idea to neutralize the acid with a wash of diluted vinegar.

at least minimized. When wood gets wet, any iron in contact with the wood oxidizes, creating ferric oxide, or rust. Tannic acid, which occurs naturally in wood, increases the corrosion and mixes with the rust, turning the wood black. Oxalic acid, however, can be applied to the wood to neutralize the corrosion and lighten the black stain.

Oxalic acid is available from paint stores or drug stores in powder form. To use oxalic acid, mix the powdered acid with warm water in a glass or plastic container until the acid is completely dissolved. Soak a rag in the mixture and apply the acid to the stain. It can take quite a few applications of oxalic acid to get severe stains out. If fungal attack has also set in, the stain may not come out. If the stain is stubborn, leave the damp rag on the wood for as long as it takes to neutralize the stain. Oxalic acid is very poisonous, so use caution and label any container you keep it in.

After the stain has been removed, wash the area with a dilute mixture of vinegar to neutralize the acid. Then wash the vinegar off and you are ready to proceed with sanding and finishing. One note: sometimes the black stains go deep into the wood and after working and sanding the area, you'll notice the stains reappear.

If that happens, complete the repairs, perform the acid treatment again, and move on to the finishing stage. Sanding after the application of oxalic acid should be limited to removing the fuzz left from wetting the wood.

Water and fungus also cause stains and are especially difficult to remove. I have had some limited success scrubbing out light stains with a solution of warm trisodium phosphate. Sanding can remove these stains if they are on the surface of the wood, but if they have penetrated deep, you will have to live with them or replace the wood. Fungus stains are referred to as "spalting" and are valued by wood turners and furniture makers for their interesting patterns. Instead of fighting stains, you could claim that they are rare and desirable.

You might think that you could use wood stains to cover up stained surfaces, but this is usually ineffective. A wood stain will simply darken the stained surface as well as the surrounding wood. There are ways of toning and staining wood with spray equipment that can hide flaws, something that is done in the furniture industry, but this method also hides the grain under a layer of pigment, much like painting the wood, and results in a bland, homogenized look. Some stains on an old woodie are inevitable and should be considered as the natural patina of an old automobile.

You may find that after removing the finish, the wood will be colored from a dye or stain applied sometime in the past. The method for removing the color will depend on whether it is a stain or a dye. Try washing a piece of the wood with household bleach. If the wood was dyed, the color should disappear in a short period of time. If the color remains, the piece has been stained. To remove stain, scrub the piece with soap and water immediately after the stripper has been removed. I use warm water with a little dish soap and a soft brass brush to help clean the stain pigment out of the woodgrain. The warm water will raise and soften the woodgrain, making it susceptible to gouging with the brush so scrub lightly and be patient. Experiment on an old piece of stained wood, maybe a piece of discarded furniture, before you begin to work on valuable pieces. This process also works well for getting paint residue out of the wood pores. Be sure to dry the wood with a cotton towel as soon as you are done scrubbing the stain or paint out.

If the color is really stubborn, you can use a two-part hydrogen peroxide wood bleach available from most paint stores. This bleach will remove all of the color from the surface fibers of the wood, leaving the wood white or light gray. The bleached layer is thin, so be careful so that you don't sand through it, which will reveal the original tint. Because it will be very light, you'll have to apply some type of stain or dye to match the natural color of the rest of the wood. Before you try this process on your project, practice with some sample pieces. It is not difficult to learn but does take patience and some skill when blending the bleached wood to the natural wood.

If the wood on your project is generally darker than you would like it, you can lighten everything with hydrogen peroxide bleach. Keep in mind that the color of old wood has a lot of character and that once the wood is bleached the old patina is gone, forever. Take some time to think about how you want your car to look before committing to a complete bleach job. If the tones are even, you are better off not trying to lighten the wood.

Bleaching with hydrogen peroxide is a two-step process. Great care must be taken to cover all of the wood evenly with both the first and second solution. Even coverage is essential, as streaking or dark spots

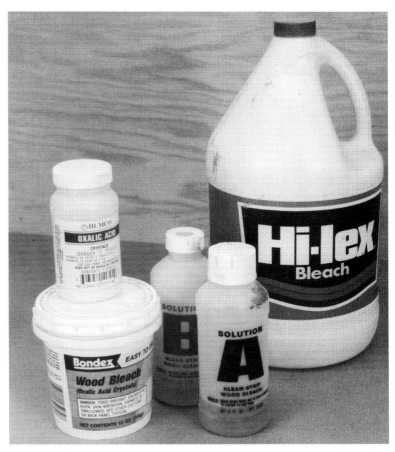

will result if any areas are skipped. Make sure you have all of your sanding and repair work done before bleaching, as the bleached layer is very thin and easy to sand through. After bleaching, neutralize the surface with the neutralizer recommended by the manufacturer of the bleach. This is very important because residue from the bleach can be harmful to the finish.

After the wood has thoroughly dried from the bleaching and neutralizing process, finish sand the wood with 180-grit sandpaper. Be careful and don't sand aggressively. All you need to accomplish with this sanding is to remove the slight fuzz left from the bleaching process.

Now that the wood is clean, repaired, and sanded, it is time to move on to finishing.

There are a number of products that can remove stains from wood. Left to right are oxalic acid, hydrogen peroxide, and common household bleach.

Finishing

Wood is covered in finish for the primary purpose of preventing the exchange of moisture with the surrounding atmosphere. No finish is completely effective at stopping moisture from being absorbed into wood in a humid environment or evaporating from wood in a dry environment. Given enough time, moisture will penetrate the best finish. The mission of a finish is to protect the wood from extremes in moisture, such as keeping the water out of the wood during a rainstorm and keeping the wood from being fried dry by the hot sun.

Wood swells when it absorbs moisture and shrinks as it dries out. This expansion and contraction of the wood results in cracking of the finish, especially at the

joints. The wood movement at the joints is more extreme because most joints have woodgrain going in different directions, usually end grain butted to long grain. The end grain absorbs moisture easier than the long grain, swelling the wood quicker.

Some finishes may resist cracking, but none are completely immune from damage. When the finish cracks, it opens the door for moisture to enter the wood. The wood swells, causing further finish damage and wood discoloration and increasing the possibility of rot. This wood movement, combined with ultraviolet radiation from the sun, will eventually destroy the best finishes. This is a fact of life with wood, and a finish that is easy to recoat, repair, or replace is essential if you want the wood to last. The best finishes not only do a superior job of protecting the wood, they also are easily repaired and refinished.

BRIGHT FINISH

Bright finish is an adaptation of brightwork, a boatbuilder's term that refers to a clear, high-gloss finish on wood. Good quality varnish gives wood a depth and brilliance that can't be achieved with urethanes or epoxies. Varnish literally brightens wood, as if it were lit from within. Spar varnish is my favorite finish for exterior woodwork, and the slight amber tint that spar varnish imparts brings a warm glow to wood.

These are the ingredients you need for a top-quality automotive wood finish. Alkyd spar varnish is still the best finish for exterior woodwork.

THE PROPERTIES OF VARNISH

Alkyd resin is a combination of a drying oil, such as tung or linseed oil, glycerine, and phthalic anhydride. This combination produces a substance that would normally be solid at room temperature, but during the manufacturing process it is thinned to create an alkyd resin solution. This solution is combined with solvents and dryers and is then called a varnish, or alkyd resin varnish. Alkyd varnishes have good adhesion, flexibility, and abrasion resistance. Most of the best spar varnishes are clear alkyd resin varnishes.

Just as water is the destroyer of wood, ultraviolet (UV) light is the bane of any finish. Extended exposure to ultraviolet light breaks down the chemical structure of the finish, resulting in loss of adhesion and deterioration of the finish film itself. Manufacturers use additives called UV filters that inhibit the degradation caused by ultraviolet exposure. Many people think that these UV filters protect the wood beneath the finish, but the real purpose of the UV filters is to protect the finish. In a roundabout way the UV filters protect the wood, because by protecting the finish from UV degradation the finish can still do its job of protecting the wood from extremes in moisture. UV light is the main cause of varnish breakdown—one reason to try to keep your woodie out of the sun as much as possible.

All finishes ultimately fail, and when alkyd varnish fails it tends to crack and check. If the finish is allowed to reach this stage of degradation, it must be removed before a fresh finish can be applied. This is good reason to keep the finish maintained. Contemporary woodie literature recommends that a woodie be revarnished twice a year. Talk about upkeep! I don't think we have to worry about our precious relics needing semiannual refinishes, but if you use the car a lot, it is important to keep an eye on the finish. When it starts to loose its gloss and clarity, refinish it.

High-quality spar varnishes tend to dry slowly. Quick-drying varnish has a high ratio of solvents to solids. The solvents quickly evaporate, or flash off, leaving a film that is not as strong as slower-drying, high-solids varnish.

EPOXY AND CATALYZED FINISHES HAVE DRAWBACKS

Epoxy and catalyzed finishes, especially automotive urethanes, are not appropriate finishes for exterior automotive wood. Epoxy is waterproof and very abrasion-resistant but difficult to repair and a bear to remove. Those drawbacks are acceptable for boat hulls and other applications where absolute waterproofing and resistance to shock and abrasion are desired. Initially clear, it tends to yellow with time but still offers great protection. The drawback to epoxy is the difficulty of cosmetically repairing scratches or other damage and the difficulty in removing the epoxy if a person decides to refinish the wood.

Automotive and other catalyzed finishes tend to have the same drawbacks. Trying to remove any of these finishes with stripper is difficult at best. Epoxy is nearly impossible to chemically strip. Many of the catalyzed finishes cannot be removed with methyl chloride, which is the main solvent in furniture-type wood stripper. Industrial strippers must be used, and they will often permanently stain the wood.

Maybe I'm swayed by tradition, but I still believe marine spar varnish is the best choice for exterior finishes for automobile applications. Spar varnish is waterproof and UV resistant, and it holds up well to everyday use. The varnish is easy to apply with a spray gun or a brush, resulting in a beautiful gloss finish. It can be color sanded and rubbed out to a very high gloss and is easy to remove with paint stripper when the time comes to do a refinish. Spar varnish does impart a slight amber tint to the wood as a result of the UV inhibitors in the varnish, but I do not find this detracting. Actually the amber tint nearly duplicates the natural yellowing of most woods due to oxidation from UV light. The yellowing is a

Spray equipment can be used for applying varnishes. Use the thinner and thinning procedure recommended by the varnish manufacturer.

warm, natural look that most people associate with vintage woodies. In fact I have known finishers who will slightly tint clear finish to achieve that warm tone that varnishes naturally have.

APPLICATION EQUIPMENT

Spar varnish can be applied using a brush or spray gun. An inexpensive foam brush will do as good a job of applying spar varnish as an expensive, soft bristle brush. In the hands of an amateur, the foam brush will probably do a better job because it is easier to load with just the right amount of material and easier to flow it onto the surface. Additionally, a foam brush can get into corners easier than a bristle brush.

Throw the foam brush away after one use. Trying to clean a foam brush is a pain. A used brush is just an invitation for dust and tiny pieces of dried finish to be deposited in the fresh varnish. Foam brushes are cheap, so buy lots of them. Keep the brushes in a sealed container away from the dust and debris of the shop. It will do your finish no good if that new brush has been lying on a bench covered with dust.

For a professional-looking finish, a spray gun should be used, and that's what most woodie finishers prefer. A spray gun will lay down a more uniform coat of finish than a brush and will obviously not leave brush marks. It is also much easier to get into tight corners with a spray gun.

PREPARATION OF THE WOOD

Sanding is nobody's idea of fun, but it's a necessary step before you can lay finish on wood. Some people spend way too much time on sanding. Excessive sanding simply wastes time and energy. All you need to do is sand until there are no visible scratches left. In fact, sanding a surface too smooth can actually be detrimental to the finish. Power sanders are a blessing, but used improperly they can be a curse. Orbital sanders are the most popular finish sanders but if not used with care they can cause irreversible damage. Orbital sanders can leave ugly pockmarks when the base of the sander runs into surrounding framework. Tipping an orbital sander can also leave gouges and sanding marks. Moving the sander over the surface too quickly can leave swirl marks in the wood. Veneered panels are difficult to smooth safely with a power sander. The surface veneer on a piece of plywood is extremely thin and is easy to sand through, which would irrevocably damage the panel. The solution to avoiding problems is patience. By the time you get to the finishing stage you've invested a lot of work and money, so take your time and don't ruin it.

Ease all sharp edges during the finish sanding stage. A sharp edge leaves nothing for the finish to hang onto. Finish will actually pull away from a sharp edge. Break the edge with sandpaper just enough to get rid of the sharp edge. This will make the piece look nicer, too, by eliminating the hard light-line a sharp edge creates.

When using a power sander, use 150-grit paper and change it often. Sandpaper that has lost its sharpness simply polishes the wood without removing deep scratches. If you are hand sanding, start with 120-grit paper to remove any scratches and then switch to 150-grit. Sand until all of the cross grain scratches, milling marks, and other small flaws are gone and then stop. Look carefully at the surface using a bright light source. Any tiny sanding scratches will be greatly magnified when the finish is applied, so be sure you have all of the marks erased.

Varnishing

Prep work includes using *clean* compressed air to remove all of the dust and sanding debris. Contaminants in the compressed air, such as oil, can cause havoc with the finish, so make sure the air is clean.

Use a tack cloth to remove the last traces of sawdust. Eliminating sawdust makes it easier to achieve a beautifully clear, high-gloss finish.

A good-quality foam brush will do a great job of applying spar varnish. If you prefer a brush, make sure that it is a high-quality, natural bristle one.

After the finish has dried, thoroughly block sand the finish until it is uniformly dull. It will take several coats to fill all of the grain. Sand most of the initial coats off, being careful not to sand completely through the varnish. These are like primer coats on a car. Clean the wood thoroughly and start the process over.

I never use a power sander to sand veneered panels. Hand sanding, using a sanding block or sanding pad, is the only safe way to sand the thin veneer. If the panels are new, they should require very little sanding to have them ready for finish. If the panels are being refinished, great care must be taken to not sand through the veneer. Sand the absolute minimum amount required to make them acceptable for finishing. I prefer to let the finish fill a bit more on panels and not sand quite so much.

The final sanding on all parts before finish is applied should be done by hand with a sanding block using 180-grit paper. For sanding into tight corners, I often wrap a paint stick or small piece of wood with sandpaper. On large surfaces, use a hard rubber sanding block and carefully sand with the grain in long, light strokes. This is the last chance to get it right, so take your time and check your work often.

120-GRIT IS 120-GRIT

I have to chuckle when I hear someone say that they get a wonderfully sanded surface by using well-worn 100-grit sandpaper. Hogwash! The 100-grit paper still has 100-grit-sized abrasive material. Just because the abrasive is no longer sharp doesn't mean that it cuts finer grooves. If you want the narrow grooves that 180-grit paper cuts, then use 180-grit. And change the paper often, so you are using sharp abrasive. Using worn-out sandpaper simply polishes the wood and won't give the finely sanded surface needed for a superior finish.

CLEAN, CLEAN, AND THEN CLEAN SOME MORE

When the sanding is finished, use compressed air to clean the residue off the wood. Be sure the air is clean and dry, as you don't want to be spraying contaminants all over the wood, especially oil. I use the same dedicated air hose I use for my finish spray gun to blow the sawdust off. This hose sees use only for spraying finishes and clearing away debris on finish-sanded wood.

Make sure you get all of the dust and debris out of the corners. I am always amazed when I see a nice finish that is spoiled by crud left in the tight corners. A dental pick or thin-bladed knife will pull any recalcitrant crud loose. This is especially important if you are refinishing the wood. Stripper residue loves to linger in tight corners. Although it may not be obvious before the varnish is applied, it will become apparent in the finished product.

A good dusting with a tack cloth followed by more compressed air will get the wood clean. I go over the wood one last time with a tack cloth right before I start to apply the finish. This may seem obvious, but keep the finish-ready pieces in a clean environment and apply the finish as soon as possible. I have seen people prep panels for finishing only to leave the panels in a dusty room for

I use clear-stain base and universal tint colorants (UTC) to mix custom stains that help blend new wood and old. Sometimes it's nice to stain interior woodwork, and it's cool to have a unique stain color. The UTC colors are: thalo blue, bulletin red, light yellow, raw sienna, burnt sienna, burnt umber, and lamp black.

hours before they move them to the finish room and varnish them.

GRAIN FILLING

A lot of woodworkers grain fill the wood before finishing, especially if they are working with an open-grained wood like ash or mahogany. What this amounts to is wiping a slurry of filler over the wood, allowing it to sit until nearly dry, then wiping off the excess. The result is that the grain of the wood is filled, making it easier to get a finish that is dead flat with no grain showing on the surface. I don't care for grain filler, or as some companies call it "paste wood filler," simply because it tends to hide the grain. Filled wood can take on a cloudy or muddy appearance, and the depth of the finish is lost. I prefer to fill the grain with many coats of well-sanded varnish. This takes more time and effort but the results are well worth it. I also don't mind a bit of the grain showing in the finish surface, as it looks just like real wood.

STAINING

There is really no need to stain the wood on a new body. The new wood will pick up a light amber cast from the spar varnish and will also acquire a rich patina from exposure to the sun. I find that stain too often hides the wood's natural beauty.

If you are doing a restoration, there are times when a bit of stain is needed to match new wood to old. I mix up my own stains in order to get the color just right. I use a clear stain base and universal tint colorants, available from paint stores, and have at it. It takes some practice to mix a stain that will exactly match the original wood, but you will have better luck making your own than having a paint store try to match it. No two pieces of wood will accept stain exactly the same, so it takes some fiddling to match all the pieces. Be sure to stain only the new wood. If you cover the new and old with stain, the old will change color, too, resulting in a mismatch.

If you have bleached all of the wood on the body, a light stain may be called for to give it some color. Be careful, as you may get more color than you expect. Maple is especially hard to stain. It tends to get a blotchy, uneven look. Try experimenting with scrap wood before you commit the whole car to a stain treatment.

PRIMERS

I usually thin the spar varnishes about 10 percent with thinner for use as a primer coat. Most varnish makers make recommendations for thinners that are compatible with their product. Read the directions on the can and follow them. Don't try to save a few bucks on cheap thinner.

Thinned varnish is the only primer that is necessary. It is thinned so that it penetrates better and leaves a surface that is slightly easier to sand. If you are spraying the finish, it will be necessary to thin the varnish for all of the coats. This will not affect the finished product unless you use too much thinner. Follow the directions on the can for spray finishing. Generally, spar varnishes may be thinned 10 to 15 percent.

APPLYING FINISH COATS

Here is the most important rule of finishing: Two thin coats of varnish are better than one thick coat. A thick coat dries more slowly. If it is excessively thick, it may never completely cure, resulting in a soft finish that lacks durability. Longer drying time also means more time spent waiting between coats.

Stir, stir, and then stir some more. Varnishes must be thoroughly mixed to reach optimum strength and to dry correctly. Let the varnish sit for a few minutes to let any air bubbles escape that may have been stirred in. Use a paper paint strainer to strain the varnish before you begin. Tiny pieces of alkyd resin or other detritus can cause flaws in the finish coat.

I consider nine coats of finish to be the optimum number. Fewer coats result in a finish layer that is too thin. More coats can create a thick finish that is prone to cracking. Nine coats may sound like a lot of varnish, but keep in mind that a lot of the varnish will be sanded off before the next coat is applied.

After the first coat is applied and thoroughly dry, sand the varnish with 320-grit sandpaper. I use 3M's RN Fre-Cut 216U sandpaper for all of my finish sanding. The paper, gold in color, is an open-coat aluminum oxide paper that does not load up as the finish is sanded. It's the best sandpaper I have found for sanding spar varnish. The first sanding will eliminate the fuzz left from the coat of varnish. Sand all of the surface until it feels smooth and repeat the clean, clean routine. Be careful not to sand aggressively, it only takes a light sanding to remove the fuzz, and you don't want to sand into the surface of the wood.

The second coat is really the first "build coat." Again wait for the varnish to dry completely before sanding smooth. Most spar varnishes will be dry enough to sand in about 12 hours. Sand lightly, clean, and apply the third coat. After the third coat has dried, sanding can get a bit more aggressive. The first couple of passes will show the grain as shiny spots. Try to sand the surface until the shiny spots are gone, which means you are sanding the entire surface, not just the high spots. Again be careful not to sand through the finish into the wood. The goal of a bright finish is to fill the grain as much as possible without having a heavy build-up of finish. A thick coat of varnish can crack. At one coat a day you can safely assume it will take a couple of weeks to get a good finish on the wood.

As you build more coats of finish, start to use finer sandpaper. The next to last coat should be sanded with 600-grit sandpaper to eliminate any sanding marks in the final coat. Start with 320, move on to 400 after the second coat, and finish with 600.

DRYING TIME

Drying time is critical. A finish that is not allowed to dry between coats will always be a bit soft. Each additional coat of finish will keep solvents locked into the first coats. It is very important to allow the varnish adequate drying time between coats. Temperature and humidity will affect drying time so use the times a manufacturer lists as a guideline and not gospel. Did I mention that you need to let the finish dry between coats? When the finish sands easily without loading up the sandpaper, it is dry.

SILICONE CONTAMINATION AND THE DREADED FISH EYE

One of the worst enemies of the finisher is silicone. Silicone contamination causes the finish to form small round depressions, called fish eyes, which are almost impossible to completely eliminate once the wood has been contaminated. Sanding will not remove the silicone, it only spreads it around, increasing the problem. Silicone hangs around for a long time. Great care must be taken to keep silicone from contaminating your project. I refuse to allow any silicone-based product in my shop or garage.

One of the greatest offenders is silicone-based sprays like Armor All. There are quite a number of lubricants and penetrating oils that also contain silicone. Keep silicone out of the wood shop. And for heaven's sake don't detail your finished car in the same space as your bare wood car is kept. Many car care products contain silicone, and the stuff will float through the air and land on the wood. Believe me, I know firsthand.

SILICONE CONTAMINATION CAN COME FROM MANY SOURCES

A friend of mine used to coat the cast-iron tables of his woodworking machines with a silicone-based lubricant. He had no idea that the product contained silicone and could not figure out why he was al-

ways getting fish eyes in his finishes. Once he read the ingredients of his spray lube, the problem was solved—or at least he had found the source of the problem. He cleaned all of his equipment with lacquer thinner and still got fish eyes. Then he cleaned everything with acetone but still had contamination. After several cleanings, he finally got all of the silicone removed and has had no fish eye problems since. Check the ingredients of any lubricant you use in your wood shop or around the car and avoid those containing silicone.

There are a number of special lubricants on the market for woodworking tools that will not cause finishing problems and will leave your machine tables slick. Use them.

MAINTAINING THE BEAUTY

Now that all of the arduous sanding and tedious waiting between coats is done, it's time to learn how to keep that beautiful finish. It will take about 6 months for the finish to cure out, and during that time the finish will be a bit fragile.

Keep the finish clean. Grime and dust will scratch and dull the varnish, so wash the car whenever it gets dirty. Use plenty of water and a soft cloth to gently remove the dirt. A chamois will do the best job of drying. Don't let the car air-dry if at all possible. Water spots can be a real chore to remove from varnish. Always make sure the chamois is clean.

Keep the car covered. Dust can accumulate during storage, even in the cleanest of garages. That same dust will work its way into every crack and crevice and not only be a hassle to clean but also be a detriment to the finish. Dust is not only abrasive, it also holds moisture.

If the finish starts to lose its gloss, it's time for a refinish. A thorough sanding with 400-grit and a new coat of varnish will be all it will take to make the finish bright as new.

After years of rain, sun, and travel a varnish finish simply dies. There is no cure other than removing and refinishing. As long as you don't let the finish deteriorate to the point that the wood is damaged, refinishing should only involve stripping the old varnish, a light sanding, and new coats of varnish. A small price to pay for so much beauty.

REPAIRS

Damage to the finish can come in many forms and always unexpectedly. It might be a ding in a door from some uncaring clod, or a scrape on the tailgate from gear being loaded. Inevitably you will have to deal with damages to the finish. And it always seems to happen when you are far from home.

A quick repair is essential to stop water from damaging the wood or the surrounding finish. It is a good idea to carry a pint of your chosen finish with you all the time. In the event of the finish being breached, apply a coat of varnish over the damaged area as soon as you can. It doesn't have to be pretty. When you are back in the shop, the damage can be dealt with more comprehensively. If only the finish is damaged, sand the "emergency patch" lightly with 400-grit sandpaper and apply another coat of varnish. Continue to add coats to the damaged area until the varnish is built up to slightly above the surrounding finish. Using a sanding block with 400-grit paper, sand the repair until it is flush with the surrounding finish. A general sanding of the damaged piece will assure adequate "feathering" of the repair, and a fresh coat of varnish to the whole piece will make everything right again. Be sure to mask off the surrounding wood so that stray sanding or slopped finish won't affect those parts.

If the wood has actually been damaged, more serious action is needed. The finish will have to be stripped or sanded off the damaged piece. I prefer stripping, simply because it will not remove the wood's patina, and it gives you a completely clean surface to refinish. Make sure you mask off all of the surrounding woodwork with several layers of tape and paper. Stripper is nasty stuff and you don't want to cause more damage. Once the wood is repaired, finish the piece as you did the rest of the body. The repair will blend in just fine. Remember, the only permanent damage to wood comes from fire or rot. Everything else can be repaired.

INTERIOR FINISHING

On the interior woodwork, I usually use acrylic lacquer. This is a furniture-grade finish that is easy to apply with spray equipment, dries quickly, and will withstand the rigors of interior life quite well. Lacquer dries fast, and you can apply several coats in one day. There are numerous manufacturers of good-quality acrylic lacquer. Avoid the "high-build" lacquers, as they are meant for kitchen cabinets and don't have the durability of acrylic.

I have also used regular alkyd varnish for interior finishing. Interior alkyd varnish is a close cousin to the spar varnish, except it lacks the UV filters and it dries a lot faster. It is easy to apply at least two coats a day; in warm, dry conditions you can even get three coats on. Interior varnish can be applied by brush, foam again, or by spray. I use Pratt & Lambert's Number 38 varnish, which is a true alkyd varnish, not a polyurethane labeled as varnish. Don't use polyurethane on anything!

Apply lacquer and interior varnish using the same techniques as you would for spar varnish. Attention to detail is the key to any good finish.

Building or Restoring
a Wooden Body

This chapter is not intended to be a step-by-step manual for building a specific wooden body. Rather it is intended to give general guidance and suggest methods for success. There are many procedures and considerations that are the same whether you are restoring a boat-tailed classic or building a one-of-a-kind custom. Anyone with basic woodworking and mechanical skills combined with patience and persistence can build or rebuild a woodie. A good support network of fellow enthusiasts can make the job much easier, so join the National Woodie Club. The NWC is a great club and a valuable resource for anyone interested in woodies. If you have a local car club, join that too. Here are the basics—you add the details.

FINDING YOUR HEART'S DESIRE

Choose the car you really want. This is a very important consideration because of the time and money involved in building a woodie. If the car does not inspire you, it will be hard to keep the project going once the restoration gets tedious.

I have seen lots of automotive projects, wood and steel, go "on hold" indefinitely because the car just wasn't what the owner really wanted. Once you own the car and have started working on it, a change of heart will have consequences. A partially built car is hard to sell without losing a lot

of money, and most of us can't afford to start another project when our resources are already tied up in an unfinished car.

It is relatively easy to restore a Ford because of the plethora of parts suppliers. The drawback to restoring a Ford is that they are fairly common, if any woodie could be called common. Restoring something like a Plymouth or a Pontiac will be a lot more challenging because of the scarcity of parts and patterns, but you will end up with a car that is more unusual. Individuality and ease of restoration do not usually go hand in hand. If you want an exclusive car that is easy to restore, find one that is complete to start with.

If you want something really unique, consider making a complete custom body. Designing a custom body will require a tremendous amount of time. Mock-ups should be made, scale or full-size, to check all the proportions before committing the design to fine wood. Details will make or break a custom body, and the best way to work out the details is with a mock-up. Original bodies can have odd design features and strange body lines and get away with them because they are part of the original charm of the car. A custom body has to be like a piece of art, well proportioned and aesthetically pleasing.

Arm yourself with all of the information about woodies that you can find. I have included a list of reference materials in this book and they contain a wealth of information for someone thinking of buying or building a woodie. Car shows are another great place to gather information about woodies. Try to see as many woodies, in person or in photos, as you can before you make the commitment of money and time. Knowledge is power; be an authority before you start the project. There are few things more disheartening than being halfway through a project only to find the car you *really* wanted to build. The next thing to think about is whether the restoration is going to be a show car or a driver. A show car must be nearly perfect in execution. That will consume a lot more time and money, and once completed the car can't be driven or you will lose your investment. A show car has to be perfect and stay that way. A driver can still be really well done, just a notch or two below the show car. But the difference can translate into a lot of time and money.

THE BASICS OF RESTORATION

When the mind is weak, the woodie suffers. Always, always, always label all of the parts during disassembly. It is amazing how something that seems so obvious

Find your heart's desire, whether it is a custom-bodied street rod, like this 1932 Ford . . .

when you are working on it can seem totally foreign six months later.

Categorize everything. Devise a consistent numbering system and always stick to it. The best system I have found is to label the major parts of the car with a letter. Use the letter as a prefix and use the number of the individual part as a suffix. For example if you label the driver's door as "A," all of the parts of the door will start with *A* followed by the number of the part. The top rail of the door could become A-1, the

. . . or a careful restoration of a stocker, like this 1940 Plymouth. It is important to build a car that you will be motivated to finish.

These interior trim pieces from a vintage Daimler limousine are fairly complex assemblies.

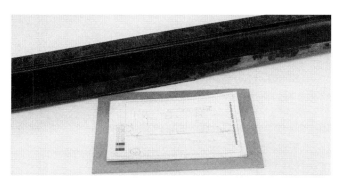

Take a photo or make a sketch of the assembly before taking it apart. This will ensure that it goes back together correctly.

There are lots of little parts that could easily become lost.

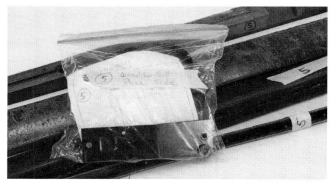

All of the little parts are tucked away with the sketch in a zip-lock bag. Notice that all of the parts are labeled with a major assembly number. This one is Number 5 on the interior map. Now it will be a piece of cake to reassemble this part after it has been restored.

middle rail A-2, and so on until all of the parts are numbered. This is an easy way to quickly find parts that belong in a major assembly, and it works especially well for small, obscure parts such as hardware and inner bracing.

Put small parts in zip-lock plastic bags with a note included as to the location of the part and a sketch of how the part relates to other parts around it. Larger parts can be stored in plastic storage bins and the major assemblies should be stored in a dry, cool location out of direct sunlight.

Take photos of the car before you start taking it apart. Interior, exterior, doors open and closed—in other words, everything. If the car is nothing more than a pile of rotten timber and loose parts, photograph it. It is amazing how little clues in the photos can help solve major problems down the road. Use a good 35-millimeter

or digital camera and take well-focused photos using adequate lighting. Take close-up pictures of details. You will probably need a macro lens for good detail work.

If you aren't especially good with a camera, find a friend who is and beg or pay him or her to take the photos. If you don't know anyone who can do the job, contact your local camera shop and see if they can recommend someone you can hire. You can probably find a photography student who would be more than willing to do the photo shoot for a reasonable price. It is money well spent.

Don't start to disassemble the car until you have the finished photos in hand. Get two sets of the photos made and store one complete set in a safe location. It is easy to lose a few photos or accidentally damage a photo while working on the car. If you have two sets, you will always be able to find that photo that shows exactly where the muffler bearings are located.

If the car is in real tough shape, you may want to photograph it before you load it on the trailer. The ride home may reduce some of the car to a pile of rubble. Photos of the complete car are preferred to photos of piles of rubble. Make sure you use an enclosed trailer if the wood is really bad. At least that way all of the parts will follow you home.

Take accurate measurements of the car before you start to dismantle it. Measure the width of the body at several points. Measure the height of the top from the floor in several different locations. Record these measurements and where they were taken. During reassembly these measurements could be lifesavers if things aren't fitting correctly.

Draw sketches of assemblies showing exactly where everything is located and include a brief written description of the disassembly/assembly procedure while the routine is fresh in your mind. I like to draw exploded views of the pieces showing where everything goes. This process of drawing and writing a description will help etch the part in your mind. When the time comes to work on or replace those parts, you will be more familiar with them and have an easier time remembering how the parts relate to the rest of the car.

Keep a map of the whole project with all of the parts numbered on it. I make a map by blowing up photos on a copy machine. Hand-drawn images will work also, but take the time to draft an accurate rendition. Make the images large so you have plenty of space to write numbers and notes. Use several photos of the car—one of each side, one of the front, one of the rear, and if possible a couple of shots of the interior. This photo-map will become invaluable as you start to reassemble the car.

If the car is in pieces or in severe disrepair, find a car of the same make and vintage and photograph it. You can also find images in books, magazines, or another enthusiast's photo collection. This will give you a system for labeling the parts you do have and a good reference to determine the parts you don't have. It is also handy to have the photos to refer to when you are unsure of exactly how some part fits into the puzzle. Make templates of the parts that need to be replaced as they come off the car. I use posterboard to make templates. If the part is complex, make templates of all sides and include the location and size of mortises, rabbets, and any other joinery used in the piece. After the template has been trimmed to a perfect replica of the piece, it can be transferred to more substantial material if needed. If the parts are in severe disrepair, it is a good idea to try and make a template for the part while it is still in one piece on the car. Often a part will end up in so many pieces after removal that it is almost impossible to put it back together to make a usable template. Here's something to keep in mind about templates: Parts on one side of the car are a mirror image of the same parts on the opposite side. If you are missing a driver's side door post, most likely you can use a mirror image pattern from the passenger's side to make a new one.

Tape loose parts together with blue masking tape. The tape stays put for a long time and releases without leaving behind a sticky residue. This is especially important if the parts are broken or fragmented from decay. All of those little pieces fit together to make a good pattern, so be careful and

A three-ring binder and manila envelopes are a great way to keep track of a restoration project. I keep photos and drawings in the envelopes and use the binder to store notes, catalogs, and other important information.

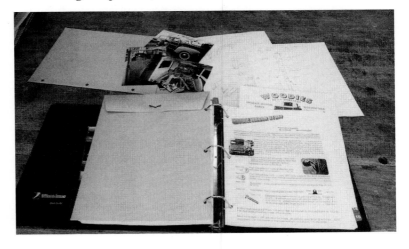

Sometimes the start is just a pile of parts. Keep the old parts until the restoration is finished. It is always nice to have them for reference. A badly rotted part makes a better pattern than no part at all.

keep them together. If the part is not going to be repaired and will only serve as a pattern, use cyanoacrylate glue to glue the pieces into a whole. This will only take a few minutes and will provide you with accurate patterns. In fact, if the damaged part is in one piece while on the car, saturate the damaged area with cyanoacrylate glue. After the glue has set, you can remove the part without it falling into pieces.

Make notes of where the wiring goes so that when it is time to rewire the car, you have a good map. Some of the wiring may actually go through parts of the wooden body, and new parts will need to be bored. It is easy to ignore a hole bored through a piece if you can't remember what the hole was there for.

Buy a good three-ring binder, a three-hole punch, a bunch of large manila envelopes, and a set of three-ring index sheets. The envelopes are for photo storage. Divide the photos by subject matter and set up the index to follow the parts of the car, e.g., door, quarter panel, roof, etc. Take the maps and drawings you have made, three-hole punch them, and put them with the index sheets. Do the same with the manila envelopes. This will give you a quick reference system with all of your photos and notes in one location. You can also include all of

your research material, such as catalogs, magazine articles, and other tidbits of information. I call these books the brains of the project, and their memory is much better than mine. These books also help keep all of the reference material clean and undamaged.

NEVER THROW ANYTHING AWAY

When a major restoration of a field-fresh car gets under way, keep everything you find during the cleanup and disassembly. Sift through the debris often found in the car and save any hardware that you find, even if it looks like it may not belong to the car. I have surprised myself a few times by finding a place for that piece of metal that looked like it didn't belong. Old deteriorated wood pieces can still offer clues on how the joints went together or where parts were located. Don't toss anything until after the car is finished.

DISMANTLING RUSTY FASTENERS

The majority of the fasteners holding a woodie together are steel screws. You'll also come across T-nuts and blind nuts with threaded bolts. Unless the car came from a dry climate, most of these fasteners will probably be rusted and not easy to remove. Wood attracts moisture and moisture really raises heck with steel fasteners.

Wood screws can be a real pain to remove. Moisture that inevitably gets into the screw holes has turned part of the screw to iron oxide, which in turn has bonded with the wood. Not only is the screw thoroughly stuck in the wood, it is also weakened from the rust. Invariably the slot in the screw's head will strip out with the slightest attempt at removing the screw.

The best way to remove these stubborn buggers is to drill them out. I take a punch and make a deep mark in the center of the screw head. Then use a large drill bit to dish out the head of the screw. I find that a 3/8-inch bit is just the right size for the majority of the screws I encounter. Switch to a 1/16-inch drill bit, and bore through the middle of the screw until you see wood dust replace the rust dust. (The dished-out head will make it easy to get the small drill centered and started.) Move up a couple of drill sizes and drill through the screw again. As you keep enlarging the hole through the screw, you will come to a drill size that will eliminate the remains of the screw, which will wrap itself around the bit. I usually drill the screw hole a bit larger to eliminate the rust-contaminated wood. The hole can be filled by gluing in either a wooden plug or slivers of wood. Such a screw hole will be as good as new again. I am sure there are other methods for screw removal, but this works for me so I use it.

If the screws hold panels, hardware, or other material that is thinner than the length of the screw shank, you can carefully grind the screw head away, then remove the hardware or panel to expose the shank of the screw. Use locking pliers and get a good, firm grip on the shank to turn the screw out of the wood.

Blind nuts can also be drilled out. Make sure you have a well-centered, deep punch mark before you start drilling. Most of the blind nuts are located in areas where you don't want to slip off the nut with the drill bit and damage the surrounding wood. If the bolt starts to spin while attempting to drill it out, especially if you have a hole through bolt already, you may have to carefully grind the head off the bolt and push the bolt out the back side.

T-nuts are a real pain to remove. They are usually hard to get to, which is one of the reasons a T-nut was used in the first place, and the wood that originally provided the grip for them is soft. Soaking the T-nut with a good penetrating oil can help, but usually there is so little good wood for the T-nut to grip that even light turning pressure will cause them to spin in the wood. Heat is not an option! Grinding the bolt head off will work but great care must be taken to not damage the surrounding wood. Grind slowly so you don't build up enough heat to scorch the wood.

THE RIGHT STEP AT THE RIGHT TIME.

I have seen too many projects end up stalled because of missteps in the restoration dance. Don't put finish on the body and the wooden parts and deliver them to a woodworker to fit together. It is easy to ding or scratch the metal during the wood fitting process, and the extra time it takes trying to avoid the inevitable ding can cost the woodie owner a lot of extra expense.

Whether the project is a restoration or a complete new fabrication, there is a set method that works best for getting to the end without major problems or the need to backtrack.

If the project is a restoration, start by disassembling the car after carefully photographing and mapping everything. If the car is a "created" woodie, or a phantom, as they are sometimes called, get the chassis up on rubber and get the cowl located and installed. With the car down to its basic chassis and cowl/floorpan, start by getting the bodywork, including the entire floorpan if it is metal, done to the primer stage.

The woodwork begins once the bodywork is done and not before. Fit all of the wood and completely assemble the body, including the door hardware and any glass that is not glued in. Start from the bottom up and work from front to back. This method gives you the chance to fine-tune the fit of the wood adjoining the metal without fear of ruining a fresh paint job. Shimming the body on the frame can help even up door gaps. Just remember to label the shims so they go back exactly as they were installed when the time comes to re-assemble the car.

If the car is a restoration, now is the time to strip the wood of its accumulated gunk and make the necessary repairs. Once the wood is clean and whole again, hang the wood back on the car to make certain that the repairs didn't alter the panel and door fit. Again, trimming and shimming can correct door gap problems and other panel misalignment. Hanging the wood on the chassis is also a good way to see if there are any overlooked repairs that need attention or wood coloration differences resulting from bleaching or sanding. It is a rude shock to get to the assembly stage of the project only to realize a critical part has been overlooked.

Once the wood is assembled and fine-tuned, it is time to remove it from the car. Pull the main body/floorpan assembly and do the chassis restoration and drivetrain work. During this phase of the build-up, the wood can be finish sanded and varnished. Varnishing the wood is a fairly slow process requiring lots of drying time between coats, so there is plenty of free time to work on the rest of the car.

Once the chassis is finished and reunited with the painted body, it's time to install the wood. This is the fussy part. You have freshly varnished wood and freshly painted sheet metal, so use lots of blankets and be careful with your tools. Keep screwdrivers, keys, and the like out of your pockets, as you will be leaning against the wood a lot and could easily dent or scratch it. Work slowly. If you get tired or find yourself becoming a little clumsy or frustrated, take a break and come back to the project when you are feeling fresh. Remember you have a lot on time invested in this project and you

don't want a small problem to turn into a catastrophe.

If you have a fabric top, install the top covering or take the car to a good upholstery shop that specializes in antique auto restoration and have the shop install it. The door hardware and window mechanisms should also be installed along with the glass, including any glass that is glued into place.

Wiring and upholstery are the last items on the list. Most woodies don't have a headliner or upholstered door panels, so the interior is relatively simple. Plywood door paneling and rubber mats or carpeting are the major interior projects. Bolt the seats in and go for that first ride. Yahoo! Surf's up, Dude!

FOR MAJOR RESTORATION, BUY A KIT

If you are faced with a major restoration project and don't have a wood shop at your disposal, the best way to approach the project is to investigate what kits may be available for the car. With the exception of tenon trimming and the final fitting of the pieces, a kit is ready to install. Some kits can be purchased partially assembled, leaving just the final fitting of the parts. This not only saves time but also saves lots of hassle, especially if your old wood will not yield decent patterns. It probably won't save you any money, though.

Buying a kit can have drawbacks. You may find that the grain matching of the wood framework may not be good. The panels may not be book-matched or from sequential sheets of plywood. Before you buy a kit, talk with the kit manufacturer and be sure you are both talking about the same quality level and that you are comfortable with the expected service level. I installed a kit that was not well made, and the maker was not helpful with solving the kit's problems or giving me advice. It was a nightmare. Ask the kit builder for references before you commit your dollars.

Kits are not expensive if you value your time. If you are working on a tight budget and have a lot of time on your hands, building from scratch can be a rewarding experience. If you are limited to the occasional evening or weekend, rebuilding a woodie from scratch can drag on so long that you will probably lose interest and the car will end up becoming someone else's project. Balancing time against money is always a big decision when building a car, and woodwork can be time-consuming.

NAMES THAT MAKE SENSE

Just to keep everybody on the same page, I am going to list some part names. These names may not be industry standard for wooden car bodies, but they will suffice for our purposes. I haven't been able to find any "set" terminology on woodie parts, so maybe these terms will become the standard.

Vertical members are called **posts** if they support the top of the car. If the vertical members are parts of a panel they are called **stiles**. All horizontal members are called **rails**. An easy way to remember this is to think of a fence. The fence posts are vertical and the fence rails are horizontal.

Floor frames and roof frames that run front to back on a car are called **rails**, just like the steel frame rails. The floor frames that run side to side are called **crossbraces**. The heavy frames over the tailgate and the windshield are called **headers**.

Floorboards are the filler pieces between the floor framing. **Decking** is the floor above the floor framing, such as found on a station wagon.

Wheel arches are the pieces that surround the rear fender and fender well.

A **doorsill** is the piece that fills the gap between the bottom of the door and the floor framing. This is often an integral part of the floor framing itself and not a separate piece.

Top bows are the pieces that span the open top from side to side (rail to rail) and support the top slats. The **top slats** run front to back (header to header) and support the top fabric.

I hope these terms make it easier to converse about the bodies. It's always nice to be talking about the same part, and it avoids a lot of confusion.

STAY CENTERED

As you start building the body, keep in mind that there is little about the body that is square or plumb.

Keeping a point of reference for measurements can be a frustrating ordeal. I help keep my frustration levels in check by using string. A tight string forms a straight line that can be an excellent point of reference, as long as the string remains tight. It can be a straight line down the middle of the floorpan or a straight line in the middle of a door opening. Anywhere you string a line, it becomes an instant point of reference for taking accurate measurements. Two strings carefully laid out at right angles will provide some semblance of square in the middle of an opening or the floor of the car.

A mason's line is the best, as it stretches enough to stay taut but doesn't continue to stretch and go slack. Clamp temporary "stakes" for attaching the string lines. These mounts must be secure, or they could move slightly and throw off all your measurements. Make sure the stakes can be positioned in their original location if they need to be temporarily removed for some reason. Make a few initial measurements to parts of the car that won't be changed and note those measurements for future reference. Check those measurements often during the build-up to make sure everything stays put.

GETTING STARTED ON A NEW BODY

The first step in building a new body is deciding on the chassis and cowl. If you are really adventuresome, you can build your own chassis and cowl/windshield frame but most of us will try to find an existing frame/cowl assembly to start with. It is a relatively easy task to find an old car with a serviceable chassis and cowl/windshield frame. There are lots of four-door sedans available for a reasonable price and they make a good starting place for a woodie.

Don't cut up something nice. Look for a car that maybe has a caved-in roof or has already been cut down for a farm truck or "joker." There are lots of choices out there, and a walk through an old-car salvage yard can usually turn up a good candidate. If you can find a car with good floorboards, that is a definite plus. If the floorboards are rusted away, they can often be replaced with reproduction steel, if the car is a popular make and model. If the floors are not replaceable, they can be constructed from wood.

There are a few fiberglass cowls available, and some of the fiberglass manufacturers are willing to make a cowl and floorpan alone, but they are more expensive than finding usable original steel. A steel cowl and windshield frame without the rest of the body does not have a lot of value except to someone interested in fabricating the missing body—a woodie!

Steel wheelwells are also necessary. Wheelwells not only give you something to form the wood body around, but they also serve as the mounting point for the rear fenders. Some woodie builders use fiberglass, but I prefer steel. If the donor car has a good floorpan, it will probably have usable wheelwells. Wheelwells can be fabricated from sheet steel.

Once you have decided what the starting point of the body will be, it's time to start designing the body itself. Collect as many photos, books, brochures and other sources of woodie information as you can. There are several books on the market that have great collections of woodie photos. (See Appendix 2.) Study those books until you get a feel for how the cars were designed. The more familiar you are with the pictures of woodies, the easier is will be to design a well-balanced, good-looking woodie. I have seen far too many woodies that have great craftsmanship in their construction but are ugly to look at. Draw some sketches and show them around to your friends and fellow enthusiasts and ask them what they honestly think of the design.

If you don't think you have the ability to make a good-looking design, copy an existing car and modify it to suit your chassis. There are many good automotive artists around who could design a nice-looking body for a reasonable price. Whatever route you take, make sure you are happy with the design. It takes a lot of time and effort to build a body and you want to be able to stand the sight of your creation.

Unless you are absolutely sure about your design, it is a good idea to build a mock-up. A scale or full-size mock-up will give you the chance to view the body from various angles and under different light sources. I have seen cars that look great when viewed dead-on from the side or dead-on from the back but when viewed from a three-quarter view look terrible. It is all a matter of proportion, balance, and lines.

GET IT TOGETHER

Once the design is set, start collecting all the hardware. Order the door latches, window regulators, hinges, and even the glass channel and weatherstripping. A good selection of stainless steel screws and carriage bolts is essential, and don't forget the finish washers. Interior lights, gauges, taillights, and any other electrical hardware should also be on hand. It is essential that all of the pieces be taken into account as the build-up progresses, so you don't work your way into any corners. You will need to know how these parts work and how they will be installed in the car. It's a pain to have to wait for a specific part before work can progress.

MATCHING THE WOOD

One of the things that can make or break a beautiful woodworking project is grain and color matching of the wood. I have seen excellent workmanship performed without regard for grain and color, and the result is less than beautiful.

Color and grain are important. If you grab three boards at random from a stack of lumber, the odds of all the boards being the same color with similar grain patterns are slim. There are many subtle color variations in any pile of lumber. As you go through a stack, separate the lumber by color. Buy a lot more wood than needed for the car, as it will give you more options when matching colors. If you have trouble seeing the subtle differences in color, wet a section of each board with mineral spirits. The color shows much better when the board is wet, and mineral spirits will stay wet long enough to match all of your boards. When the color is sorted then look for similar grain and cut, i.e., flat sawn, rift sawn or quarter sawn. (See Chapter 2.)

Try to keep wild-grained wood to an absolute minimum. Wild grain is hard to match and can become an eyesore. There is nothing more disturbing on a woodie than to have one or two wild-grained boards in an otherwise homogenous frame. They stick out like a lime-green fender on a red car.

Ideally, all the segments of a rail should come from one board and be kept in sequential order as they move across the car. In other words, the top rails in the doors and the top rail in the quarter panel should be cut from the same board and appear as one board, with cuts for the door openings. This should be the same for all of the rails, top to bottom. Doorposts should appear as if they were cut out of one massive chunk of wood. Careful grain matching can accomplish this. Again, the look you want to achieve is of a solid piece of wood with cuts for the door lines.

Plywood panels should have the grain running continuously from one panel to the next, horizontally and vertically. Buy sequential sheets of plywood, so the grain matches. Make the panels appear as if they are one big piece of plywood with the posts, stiles, and rails laid over them.

Careful grain matching and attention to the color variations of the wood will

Start at the bottom and work your way up.

result in a car that has the look of a fine piece of furniture.

START AT THE BOTTOM

Support the floorpan and frame on jackstands or some other structure that will keep the frame level and flat. Make sure the supports are sturdy, because you will be climbing around on the car a lot and you may even get into a tussle or two with some recalcitrant part. You don't want the frame twisting while you are assembling the car or you may end up with a crooked woodie. Heaven forbid!

Build the floor first. If you are lucky enough to find a cowl with a decent steel floor still attached, you are already ahead of the game. Many early woodies used just the cowl, and the entire floor was framed with wood. Some of the later cars used the floor as far as the back edge of the passenger compartment and then framed the cargo area from wood. In some cars you'll find the entire floorpan utilized.

Keep in mind that the floor will not only support the doorposts, quarter panels, and tailgate but will also need to support the seats. Build the floor using 1-1/4-inch (5/4) ash for the perimeter framing and cross-braces and fill in the floorboards using high-quality resin-bonded 1/2-inch plywood, preferably Baltic birch plywood. Use mortise-and-tenon joints to secure the

Doors are the most stressed part of a wooden body, so build them strong. This door is equipped with power windows and a "bear claw" latch, modern features that offer safety and convenience.

cross-braces to the perimeter rails and pin the mortises with stainless steel screws. The tenons should extend into the rails about half the rail's width. Cut a rabbet, 1/2 inch deep by 3/4 inch wide, around the inside perimeter of the floor framing to accept the plywood. This keeps the floor flat. Make the side rails at least 6 inches wide, preferably 8 inches. The crossbraces should be at least 4 inches wide.

If you are not going to cover the floor with carpet or rubber matting, you may want to use hardwood for the floorboards instead of plywood. Use 3/4-inch tongue and groove material, and increase the rabbet depth to 3/4 inch. Make sure you leave at least 1/8-inch clearance on the long grain sides to accommodate wood movement. The end grain clearance can be less than 1/8 inch because wood doesn't move much along the length of a board.

BUILD THE BODY, THEN THE DOORS

After the floor is framed, start working on the quarter panels and doorposts. As you install the doorposts and quarters, use temporary bracing to keep everything where it needs to be, whether it be square, parallel, plumb, or equidistant from a string line. Cross measure often to make

sure the panels and floor framing remain square. With the quarter panels and doorposts in place, fabricate and install the headers, roof rails, top bows, and slats (the top assembly). Make sure you wait until the quarters are installed to take measurements for the top pieces, just to make sure everything fits. The top assembly can sometimes be built as a complete assembly and installed in one piece. The roof rails will span the gap between the windshield frame and the top rail of the quarter panel.

The doors should be fabricated last, just in case there is some discrepancy in the final measurements of the door openings. It is much easier to adjust the door size to the opening than trying to adjust the opening to the door, especially if the door is too small.

Make sure you have the floor bolted securely to the frame before you start to assemble the body, especially the doors. If the body is just sitting on the frame during assembly, it is easy to twist it out of shape, which will result in poor-fitting doors.

TAKE YOUR TIME WITH DOORS

The doors of a wooden body are the most critical and complex parts to fabricate and fit. A door that has poorly constructed joints will sag and flex. Doors need to be designed and built to take a lot of abuse. Remember the door is only hanging by one edge and is only supported by a couple of points on the other edge. A car sustains a lot of bouncing and twisting during its life, and a door takes a real pounding in the process.

Doors also encounter a lot of stress every time they are opened and closed. Doors are not particularly light, and supporting the weight of the door framing, glass, and hardware can pull a door out of square and cause it to sag if not properly constructed. Construct the joints accurately and use the paneling and window hardware as stressed members to add strength to the door. Build them like a brick outhouse.

Use a dovetail door support in conjunction with the door latch to help distribute the load on the latch side of the door. Relying only on the latch to support the door places a burden on the latch as well as the door framing.

Design the door with weatherproofing in mind. The bottom of the door should fit against the doorsill, which will provide a place for weatherstripping. A doorstop will need to be incorporated into the latch post and a rabbet in the doorframe can accommodate weatherstripping. A doorstop designed into the top rail with another rabbet in the top of the doorframe will provide a place for weatherstripping and support for the door. The front edge of the door can be weatherstripped between the door and the door post.

Soffseal makes a number of different weatherstripping products that work well. One product in particular works very well. It is a self-adhesive foam weatherstrip that is semicircular in cross-section and hollow so it easily compresses when the door is closed against it. The part number is SRE 1085, and it can be purchased in various lengths. Nice looking and durable, it should do a good job of keeping wind and water out of the car.

The tailgate or rear doors, whichever you choose to use, have the same requirements as the passenger doors. If you use a tailgate, it will also have to be designed to hold a load when in the open, horizontal position. The lack of a window mechanism in a tailgate will allow for a lot of internal bracing and brackets that will help support weight. The inner and outer panels can act as a stressed skin to help keep the tailgate from flexing and sagging. If you use doors or a door, the design will be exactly like the passenger door with the exception of the window regulator, unless you want roll-down windows in your rear doors!

WINDOWS CAN BE CRANKED, YANKED, OR ZAPPED

Using power windows for a custom woodie is an easy way to solve the moving window problem. Stock window regulators work fine, but you will need regulators that have mounting hardware that will work for your door. Most original woodie window regulators have a sheet metal support that screws to the door frame. I don't know of anyone producing a universal manual regulator, but there are several power window manufacturers that make universal regulator kits.

Mike Chiavetta has produced an excellent set of Model A–style woodie plans that have a pull-strap window regulator like many early cars had. His plans are available from the National Woodie Club, and are darned good if you want to build an early-style woodie.

DOOR LATCHES

Bear claw latches are the best. Easy to install and very safe, the bear claw latch will help keep doors shut tight, and that makes a door last a lot longer. Tri/Mark manufactures the bear claw latch in several different styles, along with the related hardware. Many aftermarket parts suppliers carry their products. (See Sources of Supply.)

Antique door latches work fine but lack the safety of modern latches. To hold a door as firmly with an antique latch as you can with a bear claw would require a very tight fit between the plunger and the striker, resulting in a door that could be hard to close. Slamming a door closed

The "bear claw" latch assembly is a real safety feature if you are building a new body. The doors will remain closed and are better supported than with the old-time latches.

every time you use it gets old, and it's tough on the door. A bear claw doesn't have a plunger. It can be adjusted so the door closes tightly without the hassle or the plunger dragging on the striker every time you open the door.

Electric door actuators are a nice, modern touch that eliminates the need for external door hardware. Always make sure you have a manual override inside the car, so you can get out quickly if the power should fail, as in an accident or fire.

PANEL RAILS AND STILES

Most doors in old woodies have decorative stiles and rails in the door and quarter panels. These pieces are simply cut to fit and fastened from the back with screws. This method allows the door panels to be one piece of plywood, with the stiles and rails acting as stiffeners, which will add considerably to the strength of the door. Ease of assembly and inherent strength, along with light weight, make for a great combination.

TOP BOWS

Top bows have a curve to provide a slight crown to the top. The slight crown adds a considerable amount of strength and prevents the top from bellying. The top bows usually fit into mortises cut into the top of the side rails. For a stronger alternative, consider using dovetail joints, which would keep the bows positively locked into the rail. The top bows also provide a good place to mount a dome light.

TOP SLATS

Top slats are usually made from fine-grained woods such as aspen or basswood. Ash could be used but it would give the ceiling in your car a "busier" look because of the wood's pronounced grain.

Hard or soft maple are also good choices because they have a fairly plain grain. But the best choices are basswood and aspen, which yield a nice-looking, light-colored ceiling.

Use screws to fasten the slats to the bows. Flat head Number 6 stainless steel screws, 1-inch long, will work fine. Make sure you set the screws so the heads are exactly flush with the top of the slat, because this area will be upholstered. Stagger the screws front to back at each bow so you don't end up with all the screw holes in a straight line. Too many holes in line could weaken the bow and cause it to split.

Top slats are usually 1/4 inch thick; the width will vary according to what looks good and spaces out evenly. A rule of thumb: keep the slats around 2 inches wide and space them roughly 3/4 inch apart. I have seen slats that have less than a 1/8-inch space between them and slats spaced at more than 1-1/2-inch intervals. Don't fit the slats tight to each other, or you could experience some buckling if the slats expand from humidity. If spaced too far apart, they can cause problems with the top upholstery.

Make sure you rabbet a shelf on the top edge of the front and rear headers so the slats have someplace to land and still be flush with the surrounding wood. All of the top pieces should have smooth transitions so the upholstered top will be free of lumps.

THE FINAL TOUCHES

The body is now complete. Give the body a final check over and then move on to the finish sanding and varnishing. (See chapter 11.)

TOP UPHOLSTERY

The top upholstery on a woodie is very similar to the top insert fabric on early cars, except there is no headliner in a woodie. As a result, the inside of the upholstery can be seen between the slats. A layer of white heavy muslin or white denim works well for the first layer over the top bows. Follow that layer with a thin layer of padding and then the top fabric.

The procedure for installing the upholstery is fairly simple. Start by covering the car with the white material. Tack the material with several tacks above the center of the windshield. Stretch the material toward the back of the car, and when it is snug, tack the material above the tailgate with several tacks. Go to one side of the car and pull the material tight enough to get it to lay nice and flat but not too tight. Again tack the material in the middle of the side. Proceed to the other side of the car and pull the material tight and tack. Do all four corners the same way and then work your way from the corners to the middle, pulling any wrinkles out of the material and tacking every few inches. You should end up with a taut covering devoid of wrinkles. Trim the material close to the edges all the way around the car.

Using 3M's 77 general purpose spray adhesive, glue the padding to the cloth. Spray the adhesive on the cloth, being careful not to get any adhesive on the rest of the car. Make sure there are no lumps in the padding. Work carefully and make sure the padding ends just short of the edge. You don't want padding behind the drip rails or Hydem Welt, or they will not lay flat when nailed on. Install the top material the same way the white material was installed. You may need to use a hair dryer or some other heat source to soften the material and eliminate wrinkles when stretching the corners. Use the heat sparingly, as you don't want to damage the material. After the material has been completely fastened, cover the fasteners and the edge with silicone caulking to seal out water. This is the one exception to my "no silicone" rule. Be careful not to get the silicone anywhere other than where the drip rail or Hydem Welt will go. Silicone is a real pain to clean off varnished wood or the top material.

The final step is to install the stock moldings and drip rail. If the body is a custom, use Hydem Welt to cover all the edges.

KEEPING UP THE WOODIE

Woodies are not real fussy as far as upkeep is concerned. There is no need to wax the spar varnish finish. Just keep the car clean and limit exposure to the sun when possible.

Winter storage is easy. Clean the car and put a good cover on it. Keep the car out of any direct sunlight. Even with a cover, direct sunlight can still damage it. Mouse-proof the interior. You don't want mice trying to make a nest out of the top padding or gnawing on the woodwork. Humidity shouldn't be a problem unless you store the car in a very humid building, which I suggest you avoid.

Don't put any desiccant in the interior area. A desiccant can dry the wood to the point of damage. Humidity changes are a natural phenomenon, and wood can tolerate the changes just fine as long as they aren't severe.

Make sure you put as many miles on your woodie as you can. They love to be driven, and you will love to drive yours. Good woodworking!

Sources of Supply

Milwaukee Sprayer
5635 W. Douglas Ave.
Milwaukee, WI 53218
800-558-7035
414-527-0086 FAX
Sure Shot sprayer for applying liquid paint stripper

Sansher Corporation
8005 N. Clinton St.
Fort Wayne, IN 46825
219-484-2000
Dad's Easy Spray methylene chloride–based paint stripper

Woodcraft
560 Airport Industrial Park
Parkersburg, WV 26102
800-225-1153
Behlen's ground hide glue and woodworking tools; a number of Woodcraft stores are located in cities around the United States

System Three Epoxy
3500 West Valley North,
Suite 105
Auburn, WA 98001
800-333-5514
T-88 epoxy, Sculpwood, RotFix, and Quick-Cure epoxy; epoxy primers and specialized epoxies

American Saw & Mfg. Company
301 Chestnut St.
East Longmeadow, MA 01028
800-628-3030
413-525-3961
www.lenoxsaw.com
Lenox hole saws, band saw blades, jigsaw blades and reciprocating saw blades

Wagner Electronics
326 Pine Grove Rd.
Rogue River, OR 97537
800-585-7609
Wagner moisture meters

The Wood 'n Carr
3231 E. 19th St.
Signal Hill, CA 90804
562-498-8730
562-498-3360 FAX
Woodie restoration and custom wooden bodies

B&B Rare Woods
10946 W. Texas Ave.
Lakewood, CO 80232
303-986-2585
Standard and exotic wood veneers

W. L. Fuller, Inc.
P.O. Box 8767
7 Cypress St.
Warwick, RI 02888
401-467-2900
401-467-2905 FAX
Tapered twist drills with countersink and adjustable stop

GarrettWade
161 Avenue of the Americas
New York, NY 10013
800-221-2942
Hock plane blades and other woodworking tools; catalog is great resource with great tool descriptions

Howell's Sheetmetal
P.O. Box 792
Nederland, TX 77627
800-375-6663
Steel inner fender panels for Model A Fords

Soffseal
104 May Drive
Harrison, OH 45030
800-426-0902
Weatherstripping and rubber details; glass run channel for windows

Braun Manufacturing Co., Inc.
1350 Feehanville Drive
Mount Prospect, IL 60056
847-635-2050
Stainless steel continuous hinges (piano hinges)

Tri/Mark
Industrial Park
New Hampton, IA 50659
515-394-3188
515-394-2392
Bear claw door latches and hardware

Downs Manufacturing
715 N. Main St.
Lawton, MI 49065
616-624-4081
616-624-6359 FAX
Fiberglass cowls

Superior Glass Works
P.O. Box 1140
Mulino, OR 97042
503-829-9634
503-829-6634 FAX
Fiberglass cowls

Specialty Power Windows
2087 Collier Road
Forsyth, GA 31209
800-634-9801
Universal power window kits

LeBaron Bonney Co.
6 Chestnut St.
P.O. Box 6
Amesbury, MA 01913
978-388-3811
978-388-1113 FAX
www.lebaronbonney.com
Top fabric, plated tacks, upholstery, and antique auto parts

town Distributors
Vood St. Bldg. Number 15
RI 02809
3-0030
4-5829 FAX
iless steel wood screws and carriage bolts,
woodworking supplies, stainless steel
continuous hinges (piano hinges)

S&S Industries
1931 Cheeseman Hill Rd.
Delevan, NY 14142
716-535-4604
Ironwork for wooden station wagons
1928–1931 Ford and Model T depot hacks

Tim Conner
10499 Vermont Ave.
Hayward, WI 54843
715-634-3735
715-462-3756
Stainless steel blind nuts 5/16–18 and 5/16–24

Ed Clarke
67 Rockland Ave.
Larchmont, NY
914-834-0326
Hardware and restoration supplies

APPENDIX 2

Reference Books and Interesting Reading

Bloechl, Rich. *The Do-It-Yourself Guide to Woodie Woodworking.* Santa Clara, CA: Bay Area Graphics, 1993.

Bloechl, Richard. *Woodies & Wagons A Pictorial History.* Santa Clara, CA: Bay Area Graphics, 2000.

Duginske, Mark. *Mastering Woodworking Machinery.* Newtown, CT: Taunton Press, 1992.

Fetherston, David. *American Woodys.* Sebastopol, CA: Thaxton Press, 1998.

Fetherston, David. *Woodys.* Osceola, WI: MBI Publishing Company., 1995.

Frid, Tage. *Tage Frid Teaches Woodworking, Book 1—Joinery.* Newtown, CT: Taunton Press, 1979.

Garrett, DDS, Thomas B. *Vintage Station Wagon Shop Service.* Arcadia, CA: Post-Era Books, 1977. *(Long out-of-print, but worth the search.)*

Hack, Garrett. *Classic Hand Tools.* Newtown, CT: Taunton Press, 1999.

Halberstadt, Hans. *Woodies.* New York City: Friedman/Fairfax Publishers, 2000.

Wagner, Rob Leicester. *Wood Details.* New York City: Friedman/Fairfax Publishers, 2000.

Yenne, Bill. *Classic Cars: Woodies A National Treasure.* Cobb, CA: O.G. Publishing, Inc., 1997.

The Taunton Press
63 South Main St.
Newtown, CT. 06470
800-888-8286
Fine Woodworking *magazine; woodworking books, tool books and videos*

Astragal Press
5 Cold Hill Road, Suite 12
P.O. Box 239
Mendham, NJ 07945
973-543-3045
973-543-3044 FAX
Antique woodworking tool books and other woodworking books

The Fine Tool Journal
27 Fickett Rd.
Pownall, ME 04069
207-688-4962
207-688-4831 FAX
AntiqueTtool Magazine

Glossary

Annual rings: Growth rings visible when a log is viewed from the end. Each ring signifies one year of growth. Tropical woods have growth rings that are very hard to distinguish because of the lack of distinct growing seasons.

Bow: 1. A form of warp that is a deviation from flatness along the length of the board. (See illustration in chapter 1.) 2. A frame or brace located in the top of a car, particularly cloth-topped cars.

Clamping caul: A piece of wood used to distribute clamp pressure over a larger area than the clamp alone would provide.

Closed time: Length of time a glued joint must have clamp pressure.

Crook: A form of warp that is a deviation from end-to-end straightness. Like a bow, only with the board on edge. (See illustration in chapter 1.)

Cross-brace: A frame member running side to side.

Cup: A form of warp that is a deviation from flat across the width of the board.

Cure time: The length of time it takes for a glued joint to reach maximum strength.

Decking: The wooden floor above the floor framing, as in the rear of a station wagon.

Doorsill: A wooden piece that fills the gap between the bottom of the door and the floor framing. This is often an integral part of the floor framing.

Dowel: A round pin inserted into a hole drilled in adjoining boards to keep the boards in alignment. A dowel can also be used to lock a joint together, such as in a pinned mortise and tenon.

Dovetail: A tenon that is wider at its end than at its base.

Edge lamination: Gluing two or more boards together edge to edge.

Face lamination: Gluing two or more boards together face to face.

Floorboards: Wood filler pieces between frame members.

Flitch: A bundle of veneer arranged as it came from the log.

Gap filling: The ability of glue or filler to structurally bridge gaps in wood or joinery.

Glue creep: The tendency for a glue to expand past the glue joint, resulting in a ridge appearing along the glue line after the piece has been sanded flush.

Half-lap: A joint between two boards in which half the thickness of each board is removed, resulting in a flush surface when the boards are joined.

Header: The heavy framing member above the windshield and the tailgate of a wooden-bodied car.

Hydem Welt: This kind of welt, commonly used when attaching top material to the perimeter of the roof, has flaps concealing the tacks that secure the top to the woodie frame.

Kink: A form of warp that is characterized by a sudden bend in the board usually caused by a knot. (See illustration in chapter 1.)

Mortise: A notch, hole, or slot cut into a board to receive a tenon of the same dimensions.

Open time: Maximum length of time a glued-up joint can remain unclamped.

Post: The vertical member that supports the top of the car.

Rail: Floor frames and roof framing that runs front to back on a car.

Slat: Thin pieces of wood that run front to back over the top bows and support the top fabric.

Stack lamination: Gluing a number of boards together face to face to build up thickness.

Stile: The vertical member of a frame, particularly a panel frame.

Substrate: The background wood that veneer is glued to. In most cases, a lower-priced, stable wood such as pine, aspen, or basswood.

Tack cloth: A piece of cheesecloth covered with a resinous substance that will pick up dust particles when wiped across the surface of wood. Used in preparation for varnishing.

Top bow: See bow.

Twist: A warp that is a deviation from flat the length of the board. Not all four corners will sit flat. (See illustration in chapter 1.)

Warp: A distortion of the wood from its originally intended shape, usually as a result of drying.

Wheel arch: A wooden frame that surrounds the rear fender and fender well.

Tenon: A projection at the end of a board that is designed to fit into a mortise of the same dimensions.

Index

..., 134
...ngs, 58
..., 29
...als, safety, 8
...ne, 113
...an-style foot switch, 44
...time, 140
...mask, safety, 6
...uffs, safety, 7
... sawn, 9
...at-sole, 29, 31, 86
gloves, 7
half-lap joint, 67, 68
hollow-chisel mortise
    attachment, 56
mortise, 43, 68, 69
plain-sliced plywood, 23
quarter sawn, 9
rift sawn, 9
rip fence, 47
safety glasses, 8
safety, 5
sawdust, safety, 5
scarf joint, 69, 123
shelf life, 120
shop vacuum, safety, 6
tenon, 43, 59, 68
toothed rim, 36
torsional forces, 68
twist, 12
warp, 12
wood movement, 10

Types of Wood
1 Common, 19, 20
2 Common, 19
3 Common, 19
ash, 14
ash, white, 97
aspen, 14
basswood, 14
beech, 14
birch, 14
birch, Baltic plywood, 22
Brazilian rosewood, 101
butternut, 14
carpathian elm burl, 17, 99
cherry, 14, 97
elm, 14
hardwoods, 13
hickory, 15
Indian rosewood, 101
lacewood, 100
mahogany, 15

mahogany, flame crotch, 17
mahogany, Honduras, 98
mahogany, Ribbon-striped
    African, 97
maple curly, 17
maple, 14, 98
maple, bird's eye, 99
maple, soft, 16
mapple fiddleback, 17
oak, red, 16
oak, white, 16
pomelle sapele, 18, 100
rosewood, 101
sapwood, 20
softwoods, 12
teak, 16
tropical woods, 13
walnut, 16, 98
walnut, burl, 99

Tools & Materials
120-Grit
application equipment
    Arkansas stone, 40, 41
band saw tune-up and
    maintenance, 48
band saw, 25, 26, 46–49, 51,
    66, 80, 85
band saw, set up, 49, 50
band saw, sizes, 48
belt sander, 41, 42
bending form, 90
biscuit joiners, 45, 59
blade guides, 47
block plane, 30, 86
block sander, 26
board sander, 26
bow, 12, 110
brad-point drills, 35
cabinet scrapers, 38, 39
carbide, 53
carving mallet, 26, 37
combination mortise/marking
    gauge, 26
coping saw, 26
crosscut saw, 26, 31
custom jig, 67
cyanoacrylate glue, 115, 121
dado blade, 53
dado head, 69
dadoes, 43, 60
dead-blow hammer, 26, 36, 37
diamond sharpening stone, 26
doweling jig, 64
Dozuki saw, 26, 32, 61

drill bits, 34
drill press, 27, 36, 56
dual-action (DA) sanders, 43
European-style blades, 51
finish sanders, 43
flush cutter, 45
Forstner bits, 34, 35
guides, 51, 52
hand plane, 25, 28, 54
hand-hand coping saw, 85
handsaw, 31
hole saw, 36
honing oil, 41
jack plane, 29
Japanese Ryobi saw, 32
jigsaw, 27, 45, 46
jointer plane, 29
jointer, 25, 27, 54
kiln, 77
knife, 40
low-angle block plane, 26
mallet, 61
metal guide blocks, 47
moisture meter, 24
orbital sander, 27, 43
oxalic acid, 132
paint scraper, 38, 39
phenolic guides, 47
planer, 25
plywood, 22, 23
plywood, rotary-cut, 23
polyester body filler, 122
polyurethane glue, 116
portable belt sander, 27
portable work benches, 55
power bore bits, 35
power tools, 41
profile gauge, 89
PVA glue, 57, 115, 126
rabbet plane, 30
rabbet-cutting bit, 69
radial arm saw, 53
radial drill press, 56
random-orbit sander, 43
resorcinol, 117
ripsaw, 31
rotary veneer, 23
router bit, 43, 45
router switch, 44
router table, 26, 44, 68, 91
router, 26, 43, 69, 91
Sawzall, 85
scrub plane, 26, 29, 86
self-centering drill, 36
shaper, 25, 91

sharpening tools, 39
short grain, 76
short-nap paint roller, 81
side blade guides, 47
silicone contamination, 140
smoothing plane, 26, 29
spade bit, 35
spalting, 132
Spanish windlass, 38
spar varnish, 135, 139
spray equipment, 136
square, 26
stack laminate, 58
straight bit, 68
straight grain, 77
System Three, 122
table saw, 25, 27, 52
tape measure, 27
taper drill/countersink
    combination bit, 35
types of strippers, 128
urea resin glue, 128
veneers, 16
wedges, 38
wood-buying kit, 18

How-to
basics of restoration, 143
bedding hardware in epoxy, 96
bending and shaping wood, 76
building a bending form, 77
building a steam box, 79
building or restoring a
    wooden body, 142
buying wood for bending, 76
calculating board feet, 21
creating a mortise-and-tenon
    joint, 70
cutting a rabbet, 75
dismantling rusty fastners, 146
dovetail joinery, 33, 58, 60, 62,
    64, 65
dowel joint, 64, 65
doweled-butt joints, 65
doweling, 78
edge gluing, 58
edge-to-edge laminating, 57
edge-to-face, 58
end-grain joint, 59
face-to-edge, 58, 59
finger joint, 65, 66
finishing, 134
gluing problem wood, 119
grading lumber, 19
grain configuration, 100

grain filling, 138
grain orientation, 10
grain run-out, 77
hide glue repairs, 114, 125
holding the curve, 83
installing sister frames or
    doublers, 124
interior finishing, 141
interior trim, 98
laminate bending, 80, 82, 83
laminate trimming, 45
laminating a top bow, 82
laminating, 54, 58, 81
measuring, 27
mortise-and-tenon joint, 58, 67
mortising attachment, 27
patterns, from a drawing, 88
patterns, from a picture, 89
patterns, making and using, 87
patterns, of an irregular
    surface, 89
patterns, routing of, 90
patterns, using an existing
    piece, 88
preparing of the wood, 136
    pricing, 121
refinishing and restoring
    wood, 128
removing color and stains, 131
repairing and restoring old
    wood and veneer, 121
repairing bare wood, 130
repairing hide glue with
    veneer, 125
repairing veneer, 125
repairs, 141
sanding, 86, 131
sawing, 85
shaping as a reduction
    process, 84
sharpening a chisel, 41
splicing broken or rotten
    wood, 123
staining, 138
steam bending, 78
storing wood, 21
stripping procedures, 128
varnishing, 102, 104, 137
wallpaper method, 127

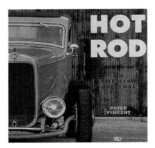

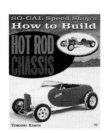

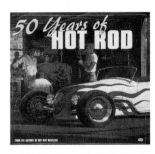
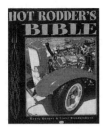
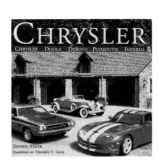
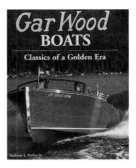
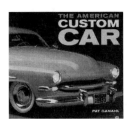